LADY HAMILTON

LADY HAMILTON

LADY HAMILTON
in relation to the art of her time

An exhibition organised by
the Arts Council of Great Britain and
the Greater London Council
at the Iveagh Bequest, Kenwood

18 July – 16 October 1972

The Arts Council of Great Britain

The exhibition selected and catalogued by Patricia Jaffé

COVER *George Romney* Emma wearing a white scarf
lent by Mr and Mrs John Koch (15)
Designed and printed in England by Shenval

Foreword

In a sense this exhibition is the fulfilment of two dreams. Emma Hamilton has long held a magical attraction, especially for those who have admired the famous paintings by Romney which hang on the walls of Kenwood, and it has been the wish of many of us to see, one day, an exhibition devoted to her. Similarly we always hoped that it would be possible to use the rooms at Kenwood, one of the finest Neo-classical houses in London, for part of a Neo-classical exhibition or for an exhibition on a theme relating to the period. Hence the subject and venue of the present exhibition were warmly welcomed by the Arts Council, who are responsible for the overall organisation, and by the Greater London Council, who are sharing the costs as well as housing the exhibition.

Mrs Patricia Jaffé was invited to select the works and to write the catalogue; we are indebted to her for the enthusiasm and scholarship with which she has brought together a most varied and fascinating selection of paintings, drawings, furniture, books and *objets d'art*, portraying Emma Hamilton and showing the art of her time and the not inconsiderable effect she had on it.

We are most grateful to the lenders who have parted with works from their collections for a long period, which overlaps with the showing of the Neo-classical Exhibition itself.

Mrs Jaffé would like to record her thanks, in which we join, to the following who have been of great assistance to her in arranging the exhibition: Dr Per Bjurström, Curator of Drawings at the National Museum, Stockholm, whose help in clarifying the theatrical side of Emma Hamilton's career was most valuable; Professor Raffaello Causa, Soprintendente delle Belle Arti, Naples, who did everything in his power to help Mrs Jaffé document the period of Emma's sojourn in Naples, and whose assistance in making available the Italian loans was invaluable; Mr F. St John Gore, Adviser on Paintings to the National Trust; Mr John Guinness, whose photographic archive on eighteenth-century characters, especially Emma Hamilton, was particularly useful; Mr Michael Jaffé, who made many helpful suggestions on the typescript of the catalogue; Mr George Naish, retired Keeper of the National Maritime Museum, who was most helpful in the initial stages of planning the exhibition; the staff of the London Library, the Kensington Central Public Library and Cambridge University Library.

Mr Gabriel White, formerly Director of Art of the Arts Council, and Mr John Jacob, Curator of The Iveagh Bequest, Kenwood, have been responsible for the organisation of the exhibition and, together with Mrs Jaffé, have arranged the exhibits.

HAROLD SEBAG-MONTEFIORE
Chairman, Greater London Council
Arts and Recreation Committee

JOHN POPE-HENNESSY
Chairman of the Art Panel
Arts Council of Great Britain

Lenders to the Exhibition

Anglesey Abbey – *see* National Trust
Anonymous 5, 8, 20, 25, 26, 29, 38, 44, 45, 50, 51 and 52
Broadlands Collection 59
Cambridge: Fitzwilliam Museum 4, 7, 9, 10, 11 and 13
Caserta: Palazzo Reale 64
Grigg, J. E. P. 110
Jaffé, Mr and Mrs A. M. 6
Koch, Mr and Mrs John 15
London: Thomas Agnew & Sons Ltd 35
   British Museum 12, 27, 57, 90, 91, 93 and 94
   Heim Gallery (London) Ltd 61
   Iveagh Bequest, Kenwood (Greater London Council) 14, 21 and 23
   Leggatt Trustees 96
   National Maritime Museum 33, 58, 70, 72, 81, 95, 101, 102, 103, 104, 105, 106 and 107
   National Portrait Gallery 3, 16, 28 and 92
   Sabin Galleries Cork Street 19
   Tate Gallery 22
   Victoria and Albert Museum 71
McFadden – *see* Philadelphia
Meade-Fetherstonhaugh, Mrs Richard 1
Naples: Comune di Napoli (Museo Floridiana) 40
   Museo di Capodimonte 31, 32, 36, 41, 42, 46, 48, 49, 65, 66, 67, 68, 69 and 84
   Museo di San Martino 30, 37, 39, 62, 76, 77, 78, 79, 80, 82, 83, 85 and 88
National Trust (Fairhaven Collection, Anglesey Abbey) 74
Norton Simon Foundation 17 and 54
Oppé, D. L. T. 55
Oxford: Ashmolean Museum 56
Parham Park, Sussex 2 and 24
Philadelphia: Museum of Art (John H. McFadden Collection) 18
Portsmouth: Victory Museum 73, 75, 86, 87, 89, 97, 98, 100, 108, 109 and 111
Sorrento: Museo Correale di Terranova 43, 47 and 60
Taylor, Mr and Mrs Jack G. 53
Throckmorton, Sir Robert 63
Whitfield, Mr and Mrs Clovis 34

Bibliography

Bibliographical abbreviations used in the catalogue entries appear first

BAILY

J. T. Herbert Baily, *Emma, Lady Hamilton, a biographical essay with a catalogue of her published portraits*, London, W. G. Menzies, 1905

CHAMBERLAIN

Arthur B. Chamberlain, *George Romney*, London, Methuen and Co, 1910

CONNELL

Brian Connell, *Portrait of a Whig Peer*, London, André Deutsch, 1957

FOTHERGILL

Brian Fothergill, *Sir William Hamilton, Envoy Extraordinary*, London, Faber and Faber, 1969

GÉRIN

Winifred Gérin, *Horatia Nelson*, Oxford, Clarendon Press, 1970

GOETHE

Johann Wolfgang Goethe, *Italian Journey 1786–1788* translated by W. H. Auden and Elizabeth Mayer, London, Collins, 1962

HARDWICK

Mollie Hardwick, *Emma, Lady Hamilton: a study*, London, Cassell, 1969

HAYLEY

William Hayley, *The Life of George Romney*, Chichester, T. Payne, 1809

HOLMSTRÖM

Kirsten Gram Holmström, *Monodrama, Attitudes, Tableaux Vivants, studies on some trends of theatrical fashion 1770–1815*, Stockholm, Almqvist & Wiksell, 1967

MORRISON

Alfred Morrison, *The Collection of Autograph Letters and Historical Documents formed by Alfred Morrison* (second series 1882–92); *The Hamilton & Nelson Papers*, 2 Vols., London, privately printed, 1893 & 1894

NAISH

George P. B. Naish, *Nelson's Letters to his Wife and other documents 1785–1831*, London, Routledge and Kegan Paul in conjunction with the Navy Records Society, 1958

PETTIGREW

Thomas Joseph Pettigrew: *Memoirs of the Life of Vice-Admiral Lord Viscount Nelson*, 2 Vols., London, T. and W. Boone, 1849

PILKINGTON

The Revd M. Pilkington, *A Dictionary of Painters from the revival of the art to the present period*, a new edition with considerable additions, an appendix, and an index by Henry Fuseli, RA, London, J. Walker, etc., 1810

JOHN ROMNEY

The Revd John Romney, *Memoirs of the Life and Works of George Romney . . .*, London, Baldwin and Cradock, 1830

SICHEL
Walter Sichel, *Emma Lady Hamilton*, London, Archibald Constable & Co Ltd,
1905
SUTHERLAND GOWER
Lord Ronald Sutherland Gower, *George Romney*, London, Duckworth and Co,
1904
TOURS
Hugh Tours, *The Life and Letters of Emma Hamilton*, London, Victor Gollancz
Ltd, 1963
TURQUAN AND D'AURIAC
Joseph Turquan et Jules D'Auriac, *Lady Hamilton, Ambassadrice d'Angleterre et la
Révolution de Naples*, Paris, Emile-Paul, 1913
WARD AND ROBERTS
Humphry Ward and William Roberts, *Romney, a biographical and critical essay
with a catalogue raisonné of his works*, 2 Vols., London, Thos Agnew & Sons, 1904

Introduction

Amy Lyon, born on 26 April 1765, the daughter of a Cheshire blacksmith, transformed her appearance, her social status and, like many a great actress, her name. She was talented and proved adaptable, retaining still her spontaneity – an attractive, vivacious, uninhibited and warm-hearted girl. As Emma Hart she learned to school her talents; and the increased powers of which this made her conscious swelled her ambitions. The career into which circumstances guided her was that of a lady of pleasure, a beautiful and pliant mistress who lived for protracted periods with at least four notables in English society, young Sir Harry Fetherstonhaugh of Uppark, the not so young connoisseur Charles Greville, the already ageing British Envoy in Naples, Sir William Hamilton, and finally the middle-aged naval hero Horatio Nelson. What distinguished her, apart from her superabundant youthful charms, was her unfeigned loyalty to each of her protectors in turn, and the phenonemal fact that she remained on relatively good terms with them all to the end of their lives. What raised her above other ladies of similar pursuits was that, after living with her under the same roof for five years, Charles Greville handed her on to his uncle, Sir William Hamilton who in turn, having lived with her for five years, married her. What might have been her fate with her last protector was never put to trial; for Nelson, having lived with her for five years, was killed at Trafalgar.

Nelson died a hero. The height of Emma's ambition at one time was to be classed as a heroine. Her contemporaries never allowed her this distinction. They gossiped about her, telling colourful tales – but always of a denigrating kind. They caricatured her. And, when all but the first and least significant of her protectors were dead, they impounded her goods and confined her for debt. Debt drove her from England to a lonely and inebriate exile. She died in France on 15 January 1815. Her life has become a classic tale.

Yet there was one aspect of her career hard to denigrate. J. T. Herbert Baily, in his charmingly partisan but prudish *Emma, Lady Hamilton* of 1905, says, 'Emma Hamilton was beautiful in her best years, of such fresh, and sweet, and exquisite beauty, both in form and figure, that it gained her an affection which could never have been hers had a plain appearance been joined to a most irreproachable past. . . . If Nelson had never loved the fair Emma, Romney would have given her a fame as lasting as the paint on his pictures. Best, perhaps, had it been for her if that were her only fame.' In her Attitudes, which were an entirely original performance, she was almost always admired, and she set a fashion which was to become as much the rage in Germany as in England. It is principally this aspect of her fame which is celebrated in the present exhibition.

In any account of Emma, the places she inhabited, and the men with whom she lived, play important parts. Supremely important are Hamilton and Nelson. Emma's simultaneous relationships with them have led to endless speculation both in genuine biographies and in romance. The perennial fascination of the story stems not simply from the development of a classical *ménage à trois*, but from the fact that in a different way each of the protagonists was a fundamentally sympathetic character, each had real moral principles, and each, despite the pressure of events, kept the most essential part of their personality inviolate.

Emma's early life is difficult to trace. She, who could be discreet about her pregnancies when most in the public eye, was so discreet about her youthful experiences that, until she went to live with Sir Harry at Uppark in 1781, we can be certain of very little. She was born at Ness, on the Wirral Peninsula. Her father died within six weeks of her birth. The widow and baby went to live with the maternal grandmother, old Mrs Kidd of Hawarden in Flintshire. The child was probably brought up there entirely, as she is supposed to have entered service at 13 as a nursery maid in the family of Mr Honoratus Leigh Thomas, a surgeon in the village of Hawarden. Mrs Thomas was sister of Alderman John Boydell, the great London print-seller, so Emma may have had connections with the London art world far earlier than any we have recorded. The next and logical step in her career was to find a place in London as an under-nursery-maid; again she went to the family of a medical man, Dr Budd. By now she was 14. The next eighteen months are the mysterious ones in her life. Between 14 and 16 she has been credited with doing many things; these assumptions are of a romantic and often scandalous kind. Among the more credible are that she worked for Thomas Linley the Elder, manager of the Drury Lane Theatre. If so, she might just possibly have met Romney at this time, since he was a member with Sheridan the elder of a small club, the Unincreasables, devoted to theatrical interests. London circles were small in the late eighteenth century. Sheridan the younger married Thomas Linley's daughter. On 20 December 1791 Emma was to write to Romney, 'you was the first dear friend I open'd my heart to, you ought to know me, for you have seen and discoursed with me in my poorer days, you have known me in my poverty and prosperity'. One is tempted to surmise that she means a time before she lived with Charles Greville.

A more famous legend is that Emma posed, lightly draped, as the goddess Hebe Vestina in Dr Graham's Temple of Health at the Adelphi. But this is based on spiteful gossip. What is sure is that, at some stage during the winter of 1780–1 she met Sir Harry Fetherstonhaugh. Thenceforth we find verifiable records in her life history, and our exhibition can begin.

Benjamin West (1738–1820)
Sir Harry Fetherstonhaugh
c. 1772
oil on canvas, 29½ x 24in (75 x 61cm)
lent by Mrs Richard Meade-Fetherstonhaugh

LIT: Lionel Cust, *Eton College Portraits*, London, 1910, p. 18, No. 21, pl. VIII.
Harry, only child of Sir Matthew Fetherstonhaugh of Newcastle, was born on 22 December 1754. He went to Eton from 1766 until 1772 when this, his school leaving portrait, was painted by the young American Quaker from Philadelphia, Benjamin West. His father, who had inherited a fortune on condition that he acquire a house in the south of England, died in 1774, leaving his son great wealth. By 1781, when he brought the 16-year-old Amy Lyon to Uppark, his house in Sussex, Sir Harry had already given his mother much cause for concern. He gambled heavily and moved in a fast living and carousing set. His protection of Amy (or Emma as she began to be called) inevitably must have seemed to the Dowager Lady Fetherstonhaugh another step on the downward path. In fact it was only an incidence of a recurrent, involuntary attraction to young, pretty, good-natured and illiterate working girls. In 1825, at the age of 71, ten years after Emma's death, he was to marry his 20-year-old dairy-maid, Mary Anne.

In the spring of 1781 he blatantly installed Amy in his house, and the first verifiable records of her social life appear. But gossip also created legends: Amy is said to have ridden horses with dare-devil brilliance, and to have danced naked upon the dining table to amuse Sir Harry's friends. In Sir Harry's dressing-room, a charming small room papered with eighteenth-century prints, Trevisani's Cleopatra dropping a pearl into the cup of Anthony has always traditionally been said to be a portrait of Amy. In November, after spending less than a year under his roof, Amy, six-months pregnant, was sent packing by Sir Harry. His high-handed methods of withdrawing from difficulties perhaps gave his mother satisfaction.

George Romney (1734–1802)
The Hon Charles Greville *c.* 1781
oil on canvas, 30 x 25in (76·2 x 63·5cm)
from the collection at Parham Park, Sussex

LIT: *Parham Park, Illustrated List of Pictures*, No. 154, *Repr.*; Hardwick, *Repr.* facing p. 72.
Among Sir Harry's guests at Uppark during Amy's time there was Charles Greville, second son of the Earl of Warwick. Romney appears to have painted this portrait of him in 1781. If so, he is shown at the exact age when he came into Amy's life. Born on 12 May 1749, he was 32 when he received the piteous scrawl she wrote to him on her dismissal, pregnant, from Uppark: 'good God what shall I dow . . . O G what shall I dow, what shall I dow. O how your letter affected me wen you wished me happiness. O G that I was in your posesion as I was in Sir H. What a happy girl would I have been. . . .' (January 1782, quoted by Tours, p. 28.) The outcome of course was that she did enter the possession of Charles Greville. He farmed out her baby, first with its great-grandmother, Mrs Kidd at Hawarden, and later with a Mr and Mrs

Blackburn in Manchester. Until Emma's marriage to Sir William Hamilton in 1791, Greville assumed all expenses for the child. Emma he set up, with her mother as housekeeper, in his small villa in Edgware Row, Paddington Green. It was sufficiently remote from the centre of fashionable London to avoid the constant ear and eye of gossip. For over four years they lived there together, Greville spending much of his energy on the education of Amy. To sophisticated southern ears it seemed, no doubt, that in her Cheshire accent she pronounced her name 'Emmy', and this, allied to the fact that Greville considered it a convenient moment to change her name as well as her ways, led to the adoption of the name Emma. For Lyon the romantic surname Hart had been substituted shortly before. (See the signature to the letter quoted above, and Greville's letter to her dated 10 January 1782, quoted by Tours, p. 30.)

<table>
<tr><td>3</td><td>George Romney (1734–1802)
Self Portrait 1780
oil on canvas, 49½ x 39in (125·7 x 99cm)
lent by the National Portrait Gallery</td></tr>
</table>

PROV: The artist; given by him to William Hayley; by Hayley given to the Revd John Romney c. 1820; by descent to Miss Elizabeth Romney; sold Christie's 25 May 1894, lot 186; bought by Agnew for the National Portrait Gallery.
EXH: National Portrait Exhibition 1867, No. 528; *George Romney, Paintings and Drawings*, The Iveagh Bequest, Kenwood, London, 1961, No. 32.
LIT: First engraved by W. Ridley for the *European Magazine* 1803; Hayley p. 123, detail stipple engraved by Caroline Watson as frontispiece; John Romney pp. 192–3, aquatint and stipple engraving by T. Wright as frontispiece; Ward and Roberts, II, p. 134, strengthened restrike of T. Wright's plate as frontispiece Vol. I; Chamberlain, p. 122, 264, *Repr.* pl. XI; Sutherland Gower, *Repr.*

George Romney who had painted Charles Greville in 1781 (see Cat. No. 2) had established himself as Sir Joshua Reynolds's foremost rival in portrait painting – 'Reynolds and Romney divide the Town'; declared Lord Thurlow, Lord High Chancellor of England, 'I am of the Romney faction.' (Quoted Hayley, p. 92.) Romney was born at Dalton-in-Furness in Lancashire on 15 December 1734. After a scanty education, and some successful but limited provincial practice in portrait painting, he had come to London in 1762. He left behind in Lancashire two children and a wife, seven years his senior, who had probably been forced upon him in a shotgun marriage on 14 October 1756, in anticipation of the birth of their eldest child, John, on 6 April 1757. Despite the stigma of having deserted his wife which always seems to have affected his reputation in social life (he was seldom, if ever, received by hostesses of distinction), his professional success was unquestioned.

Yet Romney always longed to be an historical painter. Writing frustratedly to his friend William Hayley in 1787 he was to exclaim 'This cursed portrait painting! How I am shackled with it! I am determined to live frugally, that I may enable myself to cut it short, as soon as I am tolerably independent, and then give up my mind to those delightful regions of the imagination.' (Hayley, p. 123.) He had by that time experienced two periods when he could indulge that imagination, the first a period of study when he travelled in Italy, setting out in March 1773 and returning in July 1775; and the second the period from 1782 to the spring of 1786 during which he was able to call upon the exceptional talents of Emma Hart as model. At this period his friendship with the actor John Henderson was also particularly close and their discussions of Henderson's theories and practice of theatrical realism – the school of Sheridan rather than that of Garrick – must have done much to influence Emma's concepts of ways appropriate for enacting classical literature. (John Romney, p. 166.) This self portrait when he was almost 46 was painted on a visit to Hayley at Earthem, in the autumn of 1780. (Hayley, p. 86.)

4

George Romney (1734–1802)
Sketches for 'Lady Hamilton as Nature'
brown watercolour wash over pencil,
12¼ x 20in (31·1 x 50·8cm)
lent by the Fitzwilliam Museum, Cambridge

PROV: Purchased 2 May 1874. (Fitzwilliam Museum L.D. 14.)
The trial poses for Emma as 'Nature' on this sheet are to be dated 1782. There is no reason to doubt John Romney's account, 'In the beginning of 1782 Lady Hamilton, who then passed under the name of Mrs Hart, first sat to Romney. She was brought by the Honourable Charles Greville to sit for a three-quarters portrait. It was that beautiful one, so full of *naïveté*, in which she is represented with a little spaniel lap-dog under her arm.' (John Romney, p. 180.) There are allied sketches for the various versions of *Emma Hamilton as a Bacchante* in a sketch book formerly No. 2 of the De Pass Collection, Truro, Cornwall (folios 50, 51, 66, 70, 71 and 83). The sketch book is inscribed on the front cover 'June 84 from January'. Emma first sat to Romney on Friday, 12 April at 11 o'clock, a fashionable hour for portrait sittings. Between that date and 3 August there are thirteen more sittings in the diary for 1782. To this period the present sketches belong. They demonstrate that Emma's characteristic vivacity and animation were as much an inspiration to Romney as was her beauty and her delight in acting out a dramatic story.

5

George Romney (1734–1802)
Emma Hart, dejected *c.* 1782
pencil, 6 x 4½in (15·2 x 11·4cm)
lent anonymously

This quick pencil drawing on a sketchbook leaf has every appearance of being taken from a living and unposed model. Romney evidently made the most of Emma's protracted sittings, sketching her head in every possible mood and pose.

6

George Romney (1734–1802)
Medea slaying a child
pen with brown ink and brown wash
over pencil, 13⅝ x 12½in (34·6 x 31·7cm)
oval Haas stamp in dull brown lower r
verso: circular Haas stamp in blue-black
upper l; numbered within in blue:
275

PROV: The artist's family; Xavier Haas, Paris (died 1937); by descent to his heirs (Haas collection No. 275); Mr and Mrs J. Richardson Dilworth, Jr, Princeton, 1959; given to Patricia Milne Henderson (Mrs A. M. Jaffé), London, 1962.

EXH: *The Drawings of George Romney*, Smith College Museum of Art, Northampton, Mass, USA, 1962, No. 44, *Repr.*, pl. XXVI; *Romantic Art in Britain; Paintings and Drawings 1760–1860*, The Detroit Institute of Arts, January–February 1968, Philadelphia Museum of Art, March–April 1968, No. 33, *Repr.* Romney had long been interested in the tragedy of Medea. While in Rome he had worked on at least three compositions showing Medea and her two sons at the fatal moment when their father, Jason, hurries in to attempt to save them. John Romney presented three of these drawings to the Fitzwilliam Museum, Cambridge in 1817. (John Romney Gift 10, 11 and 12.) Romney's sustained interest in the theme of Medea's infanticide is indicated not only by the cartoon (*c.* 1777–80) presented by John Romney to the Liverpool Royal Institution in 1823 (No. 13) and now in the Walker Art Gallery, Liverpool, but probably also by the appearance of his name in the subscribers' list to Dr Potter's translation of Euripides, London 1781. Romney, who could read neither Greek nor Latin, had to rely on his more classically educated friends for suggestions of classical scenes suitable for pictorial expression. Dr Potter when translating both Aeschylus and Euripides, neither of whom had been put into English before, used to send Romney pre-publication manuscript versions of dramatic scenes in the plays. The present composition shows Medea as she is described in Euripides' drama of that name. Jason, leader of the Argonauts, had succeeded in gaining the Golden Fleece through the magic aid of Medea, priestess of Hecate and sorceress of the island of Colcis. In the process he became her lover. Later he tried to make a rich dynastic marriage with Glauce, daughter of Creon, King of Corinth. Medea murdered the bride and her father and then, in vengeance, killed her own two sons, the off-spring of her liaison with Jason. Here she steps into the chariot pulled by winged dragons, the body of one of the children slung over her right shoulder. Frederick Cummings in the Detroit catalogue commented 'It is one of the fiercest subjects undertaken by Romney.' Comparison of the present drawing with the two following (Cat. Nos. 7 and 8) shows how Emma's sweetness transformed even the most gory of subjects.

7

George Romney (1734–1802)
Emma Hart as Medea slaying a child
pen and brown wash,
$15\frac{3}{4}$ x $12\frac{3}{16}$ in (40 x 31cm)
verso: inscribed at c: 'After 50';
inscribed lower r: *Fury* or *Emy*
lent by the Fitzwilliam Museum, Cambridge

PROV: Purchased 2 May 1874. (Fitzwilliam Museum L.D. 149.)

EXH: *British Neo-Classical Art*, The National Trust, Ickworth, May–July 1969, No. 34.

Stylistically this drawing belongs to the period when Romney most frequently used Emma Hart as a model. The inscription on the *verso*, if it reads 'Fury', must have been made by John Romney or another when sorting the drawings after the death of the artist: the figure is certainly not a Fury, but Medea. Because the figure of the dead child slung over Medea's right shoulder is here barely discernible, the subject has long been misidentified. An alternative interpretation of the inscription is 'Emy', referring to the sitter, Emma Hart. Romney certainly used Emma to animate a wide variety of classical subjects, but for certain of them the sweetness of her nature made her an inappropriate model. In this instance it is only by comparison with Cat. No. 6 that the subject can be identified. The eighteenth century was neither squeamish nor prudish about the association of ideas: while Sir Joshua Reynolds depicted another lady of pleasure, Miss Potts, as Thaïs, Romney frequently at this period showed Emma in the rôles of classical courtesans, or mistresses. Medea is one of these.

8
George Romney (1734–1802)
Medea about to slay a child
pen and brush with brown ink,
$8\frac{1}{2}$ x $7\frac{3}{4}$in (21·6 x 19·7cm)
lent anonymously

A sketch for the same composition as Cat. Nos. 6 and 7, this shows the technique used by Romney at an earlier stage of his process of composition.

9
George Romney (1734–1802)
Initiation of a Rustic Nymph
pen with brown ink and grey
watercolour wash over pencil,
$15\frac{5}{16}$ x $22\frac{5}{16}$in (38·9 x 56·7cm)
verso: sketches for *Emma Hart as
St Cecilia*; and two sketches for a girl
seated
lent by the Fitzwilliam Museum, Cambridge

PROV: The artist's son, the Revd John Romney of St John's College, Cambridge; given by him to the University of Cambridge, 1817. (John Romney Gift No. 66.)

Many of the most celebrated 'fancy' pictures featuring Emma show her as a Bacchante. (See Cat. Nos. 22, 27, 50, 54 and 59.) In the Fitzwilliam Museum there is a group of eleven designs on a subject provided by Richard Cumberland. In them Emma appears to model for the two leading protagonists, a novitiate Bacchante and the priestess of Bacchus. John Romney quotes Cumberland: 'A group of Bacchantes are assisting at the initiation of a Rustic Nymph. They assail her senses with wine, music and dance; she hesitates; and in the moment betwixt the allurements of pleasure, and the scruples of bashfulness, accepts the Thrysis in one hand, and seizes the goblet with the other. Triumph and revelry possesses the whole group and every attitude of gaiety, every luxuriance of scenery enriches, and enflames the composition.' (John Romney, p. 260.) If Emma did model for these designs they may be said to prefigure one of the more lamentable aspects of her later life: she became notorious for her addiction to alcohol; it may even have been an early failing. (See Cat. No. 5.) Romney never completed the painting after these designs, discouraged by the facetious remark of one of his sitters Captain Thomas Dalton. 'His too sensitive and diffident mind was apt to imagine, that where the humorist could affix any ludicrous idea, there must of necessity be a deviation from truth and nature.' (John Romney, p. 56.) 'When Captain Thomas Dalton, a gentleman remarkable for turning everything to burlesque, was sitting to him for his portrait, he unfortunately cast his eye upon a large picture that Mr. Romney was engaged with and which was considerably advanced. The subject was the Initiation of a Virgin into the mysteries of Bacchus, in which ceremony a number of graceful females were engaged. I have forgot what the precise observation was which he made; but it gave such a ludicrous, and unchaste turn to the whole design, that Mr Romney too readily yielded to the impression, and the picture was forever laid aside.' (John Romney, p. 57.) It is impossible to distinguish in the Sitters' Diaries between Captain Thomas Dalton and his father Captain John Dalton, both of whom sat to Romney. Appointments for 'Capt Dalton' appear in April, May, June and July 1782, and in February 1783. On the whole it seems more likely that the son sat second, i.e. 5, 13, 19, 21, 23 and 27 February 1783. The story of Dalton's damaging witticism may either be apocryphal, or belong to a later visit, as sketches for the central pair of figures occur in a sketch book once in the De Pass Collection, Truro, Cornwall, and dated in Romney's autograph 'June 84 from January'. The period when Emma sat most frequently to Romney spans all these dates. Stylistically, too, these drawings should be dated 1782–4.

10

George Romney (1734–1802)
Priestess for 'Initiation of a
Rustic Nymph'
pen with brown ink and grey
watercolour wash over pencil,
$15\frac{1}{4}$ x $22\frac{3}{16}$ in (38·6 x 56·3cm)
verso: pencil sketch for *Alope* (cf. John
Romney Gift No. 86); inscribed
No. 96
lent by the Fitzwilliam Museum, Cambridge

PROV: The artist's son, the Revd John Romney of St John's College, Cambridge; given by him to the University of Cambridge, 1817. (John Romney Gift No. 68.)
See notes on Cat. No. 9.

11

George Romney (1734–1802)
Rustic Nymph for 'Initiation of a
Rustic Nymph'
pen with brown ink and grey
watercolour wash over pencil,
$20\frac{3}{16}$ x $12\frac{1}{8}$–$12\frac{3}{8}$ in
(51·3 x 30·6–32·7cm)
verso: pencil sketches for a group in

either the *Initiation of a Rustic Nymph,* or
the *Fortune Telling* composition;
inscribed in ink: *No. 37*
lent by the Fitzwilliam Museum, Cambridge

PROV: The artist's son, the Revd John Romney of St John's College, Cambridge;
given by him to the University of Cambridge, 1817. (John Romney Gift No. 74.)
See notes on Cat. No. 9.

12

George Romney (1734–1802)
The Hon Charles Greville,
William Hayley, George
Romney and Emma Hart
pencil, pen with brown ink, and grey
watercolour wash,
$14\frac{3}{8}$ x $20\frac{5}{8}$in (36·5 x 52·4cm)
laid down
lent by the Trustees of the British Museum

PROV: Presented by J. P. Haseltine to the British Museum in 1914. (BM No.
1914–2–16–1.)

As there is nothing in the present sketch to suggest that the gathering took
place in the painter's studio, it has been assumed (see old identifications in the
Haas catalogue for Haas No. 365, now in Yale University Art Gallery, another
version of the same composition) that the setting was Edgware Row. We know
that on occasion Romney went there to paint Emma. (See Sitters' Diary for
1784, Wednesday 21 April: 'Mrs Hart at 10 – Edgware Road'; that day he had
no other appointment, and must also have been going to see Greville who was
then in town). If we are to assume that Emma was in the habit of practising the
country craft of spinning, Romney may well have travelled to Edgware Row
to paint her at the spinning wheel. (See Cat. Nos. 13 and 14.) The most important evidence to be gleaned from the present drawing is Emma's familiar
association with a close, intellectual, and entirely male circle of friends, Greville
the dilettante, Romney the painter, and Hayley the successful and pretentious
poet. Stylistically the drawing can be dated 1784.

13

George Romney (1734–1802)
Emma Hart as the Spinstress
pen with brown ink and brown
watercolour wash,
$15\frac{3}{8}$ x $11\frac{1}{2}$in (39·1 x 29·3cm)
lent by the Fitzwilliam Museum, Cambridge

PROV: The artist's son, the Revd John Romney of St John's College, Cambridge;
given by him to the University of Cambridge, 1817. (John Romney Gift No. 85.)
LIT: Sutherland Gower, *Repr.*

A study for Cat. No. 14, this drawing does not give the impression of having
been posed and lit in a studio, but rather of having been made in the open air
outside a simple country house such as Greville's must have been at Edgware
Row. (See notes on Cat. No. 12.)

14

George Romney (1734–1802)
Emma Hart as the Spinstress
oil on canvas 68 x 50in (172·7 x 127cm)
lent by the Iveagh Bequest, Kenwood, GLC

PROV: Painted for Charles Greville, but bought by Christian Curwen, 1788; passed to J. Browne; Anon (Browne) Sale, Christie's 3 July 1875, lot 54; bought Earl of Normanton; Agnews; Earl of Iveagh 1888.
EXH: Royal Academy 1876 (246); Royal Academy 1928 (218); Guildhall 1894 (64); Franco-British 1908 (63); Manchester 1928 (56).
LIT: Ward and Roberts II, p. 186, No. 29; John Romney, pp. 181, 184–6; Sutherland Gower, p. 118, No. 186; Baily, pp. 36–7, *Repr.*; Turquan and D'Auriac, *Repr.* frontispiece; *Iveagh Bequest, Kenwood, Catalogue of Paintings*, 1960, No. 35.

John Romney quotes the opinion of Robinson who studied under Romney about 1785: 'Perhaps the Girl spinning is the best picture he painted in this period; he first caught the idea from observing a cobbler's wife sitting in a stall.' (John Romney, p. 243.) The painting shows Emma in what one must take to be a familiar occupation for her at this period. (See Cat. Nos. 12 and 13.) It shows her as if before a pleasantly shaded country cottage door, with chickens scratching at her feet. It may have been painted partly at Greville's country villa in Edgware Row. (See Cat. No. 13.) It was intended for Charles Greville but was not finished until after Emma Hart had been sent to Naples. Greville then relinquished his claim on the painting – in the declared interests of both his peace of mind and his pocket – to Mr Christian Curwen. (John Romney, pp. 184–6.)

15
Illustrated on cover

George Romney (1734–1802)
Emma wearing a white scarf
oil on paper marouflé,
$11\frac{1}{2}$ x $8\frac{3}{4}$in (29·2 x 22·2cm)
lent by Mr and Mrs John Koch

EXH: *The Drawings of George Romney*, Smith College Museum of Art, Northampton, Mass, USA, 1962, No. 107.
For many years after Emma left for Naples Romney continued to work on, or from portraits of her. During the years when she modelled for him so frequently he made numerous sketches of her head in every conceivable mood. Of the sheer brilliance of spontaneity in these, the present sketch is a fine example. It must have been dashed off on a sheet of rag paper, no suitable stretched canvas presumably being available. It may show her at the very moment of entering the studio, a white scarf still tied about her curls, and her cheeks fresh from the open air.

16

George Romney (1734–1802)
Emma Hamilton in a white scarf
oil on canvas, 24 x 19in (60·9 x 48·2cm)
lent by the National Portrait Gallery

PROV: The artist; the Revd John Romney; sale Christie's 10 May 1834, lot 93;

bt. Norton 55gns; 2nd Lord Northwick, and thence by descent to E. C. Spencer-
Churchill; purchased from his Estate 1965 with help from the NACF.
EXH: British Institution, 1854, No. 143.
LIT: Ward and Roberts, II, p. 187, No. 39; engraved 1803 by J. Condé for the
European Magazine; and by J. Skelton, 1849 for Pettigrew's *Life of Nelson*, Vol.
II, p. 593; Fothergill, *Repr.*, facing p. 337.
Emma's unaffected sensuality, allied to an intelligent, receptive and even
calculating nature, is ably expressed in this portrait: her full and sensitive lips
contrast with coolly searching eyes. Romney suggests the constant vivacity of
her nature by the sinuous curves of her white scarf which do not allow the
viewer's gaze to rest for a minute unless they meet her steady gaze.

<table>
<tr><td>17
Plate VII, B</td><td>George Romney (1734–1802)
Lady Hamilton as Medea
oil on canvas, 30 x 25in (76·2 x 63·5cm)
lent by the Norton Simon Foundation,
Los Angeles, California</td></tr>
</table>

PROV: From a family named O'Cluse, Frankfurt-am-Main, whose ancestors
purchased the painting in Leghorn early in the nineteenth century; Duveen
Brothers, New York; the Norton Simon Foundation.
EXH: Cambridge, Mass, Fogg Art Museum, Harvard University 1930; *Opening
Exhibition*, Museum of Fine Arts, Springfield, Mass, 1933, No. 31; *Forty British
Portraits*, Duveen Bros, New York, 1940, No. 37; on loan to the Boston Museum
of Fine Arts, 1965–71.
LIT: Ward and Roberts, I, p. 67, II, p. 183; Alfred M. Frankfurter, in *Art News*,
13 April 1940, p. 9; Margaret Miller, in *Apollo*, June 1940, pp. 166–7; Helen
Comstock, in *Connoisseur*, July 1940, pp. 28–9; Alfred M. Frankfurter, in *Art
News*, March 1946, p. 64, *Repr.* on front cover in colour; Sidney Tillim, in *Arts*,
November 1960, p. 57; Mark Roskill, in *Art News*, November 1960, p. 13;
Alfred M. Frankfurter, in *Art News*, September 1961, p. 56, *Repr.* p. 37 in colour.
No finished composition incorporating this head is known. However, it seems
likely that it was intended for Medea. In a sketch book purchased by Fairfax
Murray at the Miss Romney Sale in 1894 (now in the Folger Shakespeare
Library, Washington DC), there is Romney's draft of a letter to Emma after
she had taken up residence in Naples. The fair copy, if sent, must have gone to
her from Eartham in August 1786. In it he tells her 'I have now a great number
of Ladys of fashion setting to me since you left England, but all fall far short of
the Sempstress. Indeed it is the Sun of my Hemispheer, and they are the
twinkling stars. When I return to London I intend to finish the Cassandra and
the picture of Sensibility. The Bacanalian picture is in *status quo*, also the
Serena and the Cibele, and the Medea the last is the figure sitting with her
hair floating in the air.' (Retranscribed from the Folger sketch book by the
present writer in 1959, but first published by Ward and Roberts, I, p. 67.) In
1904 when Humphry Ward and William Roberts published their *Catalogue
Raisonné* this present painting had been lost sight of. (See Ward and Roberts, II,
p. 183.) However much her acting in the 'Attitudes' might later produce
terror or tears, her face alone was not an appropriate vehicle for ferocity.
(See notes on Cat. No. 7.)

George Romney (1734–1802)
18   Lady Hamilton as Miranda
oil on canvas 14⅛ x 15 9/16 in (36 x 39·6cm)
lent by the Philadelphia Museum of Art,
John H. McFadden Collection

PROV: Family of the artist; Mr Tankerville Chamberlayne; John H. McFadden, Philadelphia; and thence to the Philadelphia Museum of Art.
EXH: London, British Institution, 1864 (lent by the Revd Romney); *The Drawings of George Romney*, Smith College Museum of Art, Northampton, Mass, USA, 1962, No. 108; *Romantic Art in Britain; Paintings and Drawings 1760–1860*, The Detroit Institute of Arts, January–February 1968, Philadelphia Museum of Art, March–April 1968, No. 35, *Repr.*
LIT: Ward and Roberts, I, p. 184; Cat. No. 18b (as head of Miranda); John Romney, p. 194; Chamberlain, p. 318, *Repr.* facing p. 234 (as *Lady Hamilton 'as a Child' (Unfinished Study)*); W. Roberts, McFadden Collection Catalogue, London, 1917, p. 71 (as 'Head of Lady Hamilton'); Holmström, *Repr.* Fig. 52. This head study, traditionally and convincingly identified as of Emma Hart under her later and more celebrated title 'Lady Hamilton' must have been made *c.* 1785 and later used by Romney in several versions of his *Tempest* composition for the Boydell Shakespeare Gallery. The Shakespeare Gallery enterprise was launched in November 1786. (Hayley, p. 109.) Saddened by Emma's departure for Naples, Romney sought relief by throwing himself with great energy into the scheme. In almost every projected work for the Shakespeare Gallery he translated sketches and memories of Emma into Shakespearean mould. In this instance he made several oil studies from the original sketch, varying the pose. At each successive remove from this original the depiction of Miranda's terrified pleading became more and more intense. (See Cat. No. 19.) By the time that Caroline Watson engraved the head for Hayley's *Life of Romney* (facing p. 141) the image was so far removed from the freshness and appeal we see here that John Romney had every justification for complaining that engravers had never done justice to his father's work. (John Romney, p. 194.)

George Romney (1734–1802)
19   Head of Emma as Miranda
oil on canvas, 13 x 11⅞ in (33 x 30·2cm)
lent by Sabin Galleries, Cork Street, London

PROV: The Revd Wray Hunt, Trowell Rectory, Nottingham.
EXH: Royal Academy, Old Masters, 1895, No. 21.
An attractive sketch reversing Cat. No. 18, presumably while Romney was working 1786–7 on his preliminary compositions of the *Storm scene in the Tempest* for the Boydell Shakespeare Gallery. Miranda pleads with her father, Prospero, to save the lives of the mariners on the sinking ship, wrecked by the storm he has raised.

George Romney (1734–1802)
Lady Hamilton as a supplicant
oil on canvas, 22½ x 20½in (57·1 x 52cm)
lent anonymously

EXH: *George Romney, Paintings and Drawings*, The Iveagh Bequest, Kenwood, London, 1961, No. 35, *Repr.*
LIT: Chamberlain, p. 315, *Repr.* facing p. 215 (before restoration); Baily, *Repr.* facing p. 100 (before restoration).

Another fine example of a head study showing Emma in a fashionable Greuze-like pose. It has added fascination in that another artist, the little known Henry Tomson, was also moved by Romney's own urge to make these powerful head studies of Emma into full-scale paintings. He incorporated the present sketch in a full length canvas and, over-painting the pink draperies, transformed the head into that of a Nun at prayer. (See reproductions in Baily and Chamberlain.) So successful was he that even the sensitive and perceptive Chamberlain was taken in, and referred to the full-length as 'One of the most elaborate of these pictures. . . .'; treating it as entirely by Romney's hand. It was not until the late Horace Buttery was asked to clean the painting that the nineteenth-century additions were recognised, and the painting reduced to its original form.

George Romney (1734–1802)
Lady Hamilton at prayer
oil on canvas, 33 x 25in (83·8 x 63·5cm)
lent by the Iveagh Bequest, Kenwood, GLC

PROV: W. Rawlinson, Romney's great-grandson; Earl of Iveagh, 1889.
EXH: Grafton Gallery 1894, No. 82; Birmingham 1903, No. 46; Royal Academy 1928, No. 230; Manchester 1928, No. 37.
LIT: Ward and Roberts, II, p. 185, No. 24B; Chamberlain, pp. 116, 315; Sir Herbert Maxwell, *Romney*, 1902, *Repr.* p. 64.

Emma in a Greuze-like pose, this painting was formerly called 'St Cecilia' without any apparent reason apart from the intense religiosity of expression. We know that Romney admired the work of Greuze, whom he may have met on his first trip to Paris in 1764. Certainly when he made a brief excursion to Paris with William Hayley and the Revd Thomas Carwardine in August 1790, Greuze dined with him there. (Hayley, p. 148.) Romney may have esteemed Emma's looks even more because of their obvious similarity to the type of beauty which Greuze had made fashionable. It should also be noticed that her small receding chin was her worst feature, and a pose with the chin in the air – the pose so often chosen for her by Romney – minimised this defect. No doubt Greville thought it educative for Emma to practise attitudes of piety and innocence.

George Romney (1734–1802)
Lady Hamilton
oil on canvas, 19½ x 15¾in (49·5 x 40cm)
lent by the Trustees of the Tate Gallery

PROV: Robert Vernon Gift to the National Gallery 1847; transferred to the

Tate Gallery 1919. (Tate Gallery No. 312.)

LIT: George Paston, *George Romney*, 1903, *Repr.* facing p. 52; Ward and Roberts, I, at head of Preface, p.v.

This painting of Emma, hitherto regarded as a study for a Bacchante with apparently no better reason than that her shoulder is bare, is more likely to be a fragment from the composition referred to by John Romney as *Fortune Telling*. (John Romney, p. 260.) There are drawings for the composition in the Fitzwilliam Museum, Cambridge. (John Romney Gift Nos. 75 and 76; related sketches are in the Folger Shakespeare Library, Washington DC, Nos. LBV 60 and LBV 61; see also sketch book formerly No. 2 in the De Pass Collection, Truro, Cornwall, folios 78, 79 and 80). *Fortune Telling* is identified by John Romney in his catalogue of the drawings which he presented to Cambridge University in 1817. It has much in common with the composition for the *Initiation of a Rustic Nymph* (see Cat. Nos. 9, 10 and 11) although the majority of sketches show the action moving in the opposite direction from the *Initiation* (i.e. from left to right). As the two compositions are exactly comparable in style and are always found in association (see verso of Cat. No. 11) they may always have been planned as pendants. *Fortune Telling*, in a landscape setting, shows a gipsy seated at the extreme right, while two figures urge forward towards her, a couple of bashful country girls, their hands extended as if to have their palms read. The present head seems to have been cut out of a larger canvas and an extensive area of paint at the extreme right behind the figure appears to have been blocked in, suggesting to this cataloguer that the head of the background figure urging the girl forwards may have been painted out.

<table>
<tr><td>23</td><td>

George Romney (1734–1802)
Lady Hamilton
oil on canvas, 30 x 25in (76·2 x 63·5cm)
lent by the Iveagh Bequest, Kenwood, GLC
</td></tr>
</table>

PROV: Count Platoff; his granddaughter Countess Platoff; bt. from her in Paris by the Earl of Iveagh 1891.

EXH: Royal Academy 1928, No. 235; Manchester 1928, No. 25.

LIT: Ward and Roberts, II, p. 123, No. 2 (the portrait of Mrs Ann Pitt is *Repr.*, I, p. 102); *Iveagh Bequest, Kenwood, Catalogue of Paintings*, 1960, No. 38.

A fresh and live version of Romney's portrait of Mrs Ann Pitt, painted in 1788, this must either be a second version of that portrait from Romney's own hand or, which is more likely, a sketch of Emma made *c.* 1785 on which the portrait of Mrs Pitt was later modelled. Although the hairstyle and pose are the same, the morphology in this and the acknowledged portrait of Mrs Pitt (*Repr.* Ward and Roberts, I, facing p. 102) is different. The likeness of the present portrait to Emma has always been noticed: an engraving made of it in 1902 by William Henderson is entitled 'Mrs Ann Pitt personating Lady Hamilton as Mirth'. For many years Kenwood has offered for sale a postcard whose identification, *Lady Hamilton*, has rarely been questioned.

	George Romney (1734–1802)
24	Emma Hamilton as Ariadne
	oil on canvas, 31 x 26in (78·7 x 66cm)
	from the collection at Parham Park, Sussex

LIT: *Parham Park, Illustrated List of Pictures*, No. 163.

The long established practice of inventing classical titles for portraits of Emma is exemplified in the present painting. Emma is shown seated with closed eyes, her hands folded together, and a patient, rather sad expression. She is in a cave, or at least beneath a cliff. The sea lies beyond and there is the distant prospect of a sailing ship. She can hardly be said to represent the classical princess, Ariadne, who first helped Theseus to escape from the maze of the Minotaur, and later was abandoned by him on the island of Naxos, for Emma is wearing a contemporary long-sleeved dress, sash, scarf and straw hat. In the light of Emma's later liaison with Nelson, this portrait began to remind people of the fate of Ariadne: ironically the abandoned Ariadne was discovered and borne off by Bacchus, while Emma, bereft of Nelson and her other closest friends, became an inebriate.

There is a copy of the portrait in the National Maritime Museum, Greenwich.

	George Romney (1734–1802)
25	Emma Hart as Thetis pleading
Plate I	with Achilles before Troy
	oil on canvas,
	95 x 80½in (241·3 x 204·5cm)
	lent anonymously

PROV: Mrs Robertson, Struan, Perthshire; sale Christie's 1848 (miscatalogued as *Aeneas rescued from Achilles by Venus* by Reynolds), but bought in; G. H. D. Burroughs, acquired at least as early as 1868; sold Christie's; Mrs Thaw, Paris and New York, acquired 1908; Count Marczéllus von Nemes.

LIT: William Roberts, *Connoisseur*, Feb. 1928, *Repr.* (having been seen by him in New York in 1915).

Romney's 'fancy' pictures were very little known in his lifetime, painted for his own delight rather than on commission. If they left his painting room they did so with very little record – regular sitters' diaries and accounts show no trace of them. Yet as he aspired to being a history painter, the present canvas must represent his ideal achievement. It shows Thetis, daughter of Poseidon, pleading with her son Achilles for the body of Hector. Achilles, having killed Hector in revenge for the death of Patroclus, tied the Prince's body behind his chariot and hauled it daily about the walls of Troy. At length the gods became angry at his impiety and sent Thetis to tell him he must surrender the body for honourable burial.

The composition, for which no drawing has so far come to light, is comparable to subjects worked on by Romney in the late 1770s, particularly the *Dream of Darius*. It seems likely that Romney revised and adapted compositional ideas already worked on, and painted the present subject in the early 1780s when he had Emma Hart to inspire him. We know that for years to come he was to draw on sketches made of her at this period, so it is not surprising that the pleading figure of Thetis has so much in common with that of Miranda in the *Tempest* painting which he finished for the Boydell Shakespeare Gallery in

1790. (See Cat. Nos. 18 and 19.)

The pair of magic horses given to Thetis by Poseidon are represented in the painting by zebras – inspired presumably by a pair which was in the Royal Menagerie.

26
William Hayley
The Triumphs of Temper
Sixth edition, London, Cadell, 1788
8vo., calf, gilt
lent anonymously

William Hayley is best remembered for his didactic poem, *The Triumphs of Temper*. In it he instructs young ladies, in allegorical fashion, how to remain sweet natured and good tempered. He wrote it in the summer of 1780, and subsequently Romney worked on illustrations of it. The present edition was the first to have plates and these, curiously, are all ascribed to Stothard, although several of them are demonstrably of Romney's invention. (See for instance plates facing pp. 4, 12 and 57.) Romney several times painted Emma as the poem's heroine, Serena. (See letter quoted in notes to Cat. No. 17.) The best known today is *Serena in the Boat of Apathy* shown in the 1961 *George Romney, Paintings and Drawing* exhibition at Kenwood, No. 34, *Repr.*; it appears as the plate facing p. 57 in the present volume.

Emma was always grateful to Hayley for the lessons which she said she learnt from reading *The Triumphs of Temper*. Writing to Romney from Caserta on 20 December 1791 she said, 'Give my love to Mr Hayley, tell him I shall be glad to see him at Naples . . . I am always reading his *Triumphs of Temper*; it was that that made me Lady H., for, God knows, I had for five years enough to try my temper, and I am affraid if it had not been for the good example Serena taught me, my girdle would have burst, and if it had I had been undone, for Sir W. minds more temper than beauty. He, therefore, wishes Mr Hayley would come, that me might thank him for his sweet-tempered wife. I swear to you I have never been once out of humour since the 6th of last September.' (Morrison, I, pp. 158–9.)

27
John Raphael Smith (1752–1812)
Emma Hart as a Bacchante
mezzotint after Reynolds
plate marks,
14⅞ x 10⅞in (37·8 x 27·6cm)
inscribed: *Painted by Sir Joshua Reynolds*
. . . Engrav'd by J. R. Smith Mezzotinto
Engraver to His Royal Highness the Prince
of Wales . . . Publish'd Sept. 6 1784 by
J. R. Smith No. 283 Oxford Street
second state
lent by the Trustees of the British Museum

LIT: Baily, p. 126.

Reynolds painted Emma in 1784 and exhibited the portrait at the Royal Academy Exhibition of that year (No. 342). Smith's mezzotint was made immediately afterwards. His interpretation of her is more coy and less soulful than Romney's.

28
David Allen (1744–96)
The Right Honourable Sir
William Hamilton KB 1775
oil on canvas, 89 x 71 in (226 x 180·3cm)
inscribed: (lower l as if on a letter)
*Painted by D. Allen/and by him humbly
presented/to the British Museum/Anno Dom.
1775*
lent by the National Portrait Gallery

PROV: The Artist; presented by him to the British Museum in 1775; transferred to the National Portrait Gallery in 1879 (No. 589).

EXH: *Angelika Kauffmann und ihre Zeitgenossen*, Ampt der Landeshauptstadt, Bregenz, July–October 1968; Vienna, November–February 1968/9, Cat. No. 106 *Repr.*

LIT: B. Skinner, 'A Scottish Catalyst', *Country Life*, 19 August 1965, *Repr.*; O. Warner, *A Portrait of Lord Nelson*, 1958, p. 278, *Repr.*; Fothergill, *Repr.* facing p. 193.

Emma met Sir William Hamilton, uncle of Charles Greville, on his return to England in the summer of 1783. Sir William's first wife, Catherine, had died on 25 August the previous year and one of his reasons for applying for leave of absence was to bring her body home for interment on her estate in Wales. Their marriage had been childless; and as Greville was his favourite nephew and chosen heir, Sir William soon went to visit him in Edgware Row. He was then almost 54. Nine years earlier when his fellow Scot, David Allen, had painted this portrait he already looked an aloof and ageing man, though one of elegance and intellectual distinction. Here he wears the robes he was entitled to as a Knight of the Bath; in his hands he holds a manuscript; and behind him one can glimpse a case of the great antique vases of which he was already a famous collector. The Trustees of the British Museum had bought his first collection of vases in 1772 to form the basis of the Department of Greek and Roman Antiquities. This celebrated purchase prompted Allen's gift of the portrait. Through the canopied window can be seen a view of Vesuvius indicating Naples as the supposed setting, and reminding the viewer that Sir William was also the greatest expert on the volcanoes of Naples and Sicily. Sir William had been British Envoy in Naples since November 1764.

His gaunt figure and long boney face can have done nothing to soften the aura of superiority and erudition by which Emma must have felt intimidated on first acquaintance with Sir William. Yet such was his courtesy and her charm that they were soon sending friendly messages to each other at second hand, through Greville's correspondence. In 1783 both Sir William and Emma sat to Romney for their separate portraits. That Sir William was a man of regular habits is indicated by the fact that he always sat to Romney at 12 o'clock. He was, when he met Emma, a man whose schedules had been upset by the death of his wife; and he was a man for whom the immediate pangs of bereavement had already worn off.

29

Sir Joshua Reynolds (1723–92)
Sketch for portrait of Sir William Hamilton
oil on paper maroufflé,
15¼ x 12in (38·7 x 30·5cm)
lent anonymously

A sketch for Reynolds' portrait of Sir William, painted in 1777, and now in the National Portrait Gallery. Reynolds' portrait is less formal but less penetrating than Allen's; it does suggest that Sir William was capable of unbending. This is the man who could soon refer to Emma as 'the Fair Tea-Maker of Edgware Row'. (Fothergill, p. 201.) It may have been the unexpected success of the meetings between these two totally different people that sowed the ideas of disposing of Emma to his uncle in Charles Greville's head.

Protegée of William Hamilton

Having lived with her for three years in his house in Edgware Row, Greville appears to have been assailed forcibly by every misgiving he had dismissed at the outset of his liaison with Emma. The real reason may never be known. Certainly Emma had proved a handsome, loving and loyal companion. She had also proved, within the limits of her abilities, an apt pupil: she had made progress in music, household management and, probably, French. But Greville was never a man to whom marriage seemed an essential ingredient of life. He would have had no objection to marrying an heiress, but a suitable one never fell to his lot. No woman ever attracted him as a wife on her own merits. He died, a bachelor, in his own house at Paddington Green on 23 April 1809.

Perhaps Emma was for him an experiment, a trial run to see whether – should an heiress appear – he could tolerate matrimony as a means of improving his fortune. Perhaps by 1785, fond as he was of Emma, he found the shackles becoming intolerable: he probably longed to have his own house to himself again. Whatever his true feelings, he persuaded himself that finance was the true reason making it imperative that he part with Emma. He hit upon the brilliant idea of sending her out to his uncle. Hamilton had already shown his enthusiasm by ordering, and paying for, Romney's portrait of her as a Bacchante. On 10 March 1785 Greville wrote his suggestion to Hamilton in a letter which makes it seem that the idea of Emma's being an experiment is a just one: 'the limited experiment I make I know to succeed, altho' from poverty it cannot last. If you did not chuse a wife, I wish the tea-maker of Edgware Row was yours, if I could without banishing myself from a visit to Naples.' (Morrison, I, p. 136.) It took almost a year to persuade Hamilton, although Greville used every argument he could.

An additional reason for Greville's urging Emma on his uncle was that, as Sir William's heir, it was in his interests to see that Sir William did not remarry. Hamilton himself made no secret of the matter and shrewdly outlined the position to his nephew on 1 June 1785: 'Was I to die this moment my Will, which I made in England and left with Hamilton of Lincoln's Inn and brought a Copy here, would show that you are the person I esteem most – but I never meant to tell you so as the changes in this life are so various that no one can answer for himself from one moment to another. For example, had I married Lady C, which might have happened, it must have been a cruel disappointment to you, after having declared you my heir.' (BM Add. MSS. 42071.) The real cruelty of the situation, apart from Greville's cool disregard of Emma's genuine love for him, was that while she obviously longed for marriage and security, Greville could ship her out to Hamilton happy in the belief that his uncle never could consider marrying her. He sent her without compunction, but with protestations of altruism, into what might have been for her perpetual limbo.

Greville never admitted to Emma what rôle he had planned for her in Italy.

Instead she was persuaded that while he travelled on a protracted business trip to the north, she should go to visit Sir William Hamilton in Naples, and spend six months there, having her voice trained. Her trunk was packed up and sent in advance; then at the end of the second week in March (having managed to fit in two last sittings to Romney on 1 and 8 March) she set out with her mother and the painter, Gavin Hamilton, who was to accompany them as far as Geneva.

From the letters which she sent to Greville soon after her arrival in Naples one gains the impression that Emma was a self-centred gossip rather than a sightseer. Obviously she was genuinely heartbroken to be parted from Greville. On 30 April she wrote: 'I love you to that degree that at this time their is not a hardship upon hearth, either of poverty, hunger, cold, death, or even to walk barefooted to Scotland to see you, but what I would undergo. Therefore, my dear, dear Greville, if you do love me, for God sake & for my sake, try all you can to come hear as soon as possible . . . I respect Sr. Wm. I have a great regard for him as the uncle & friend of you & he loves me, Greville, but he can never be any thing nearer to me than your Uncle & my sincere friend, he never can be my lover. You do not know how good Sr. Wm. is to me, he is doing everything he can to make me happy, he as never dined out since I came hear & endeed to spake the truth he is never out of my sight, he breakfastes, dines, supes, & is constantly by me, looking in my face, I cant stir a hand, a legg, or foot but what he is marking as graceful & fine, & I am sorry to say it, but he loves me now as much as every he could Lady Bolingbroke, endeed, I am sorry, for I canot make him happy, I can be civil, oblidging, & I do try to make my self as agreeable as I can to him, but I belong to you, Greville & to you onely will I belong & nobody shall be your heir apearant.' (Morrison, I, p. 150.) It was an appeal to Greville's affection, to his loyalty, and to his jealousy. It had no effect. Greville probably reflected that his plan to prevent Sir William's remarrying was working to perfection.

But if Greville never came to Naples to collect her, neither did Emma ever walk barefoot to Scotland.

30

Bastiaen Stopendaal (1636–1707)
Topographical view of Naples
and its surroundings taken from
the bay
etching
plate marks,
17 x 40½in (43·2 x 102·9cm)
inscribed: 1659 . . . *NAPOLI* . . .
Bastiaen Stopendaal fecit aqua forti

lent by the Museo di San Martino, Naples

PROV: Acquired in 1898 from the Libreria Loeschi in Naples.

EXH: *L'Arte e la Citta,* Brussels, 1963.

Naples has one of the most beautiful settings in the whole of the Mediterranean. It is built around the shores of a magnificent bay from which climbs romantic, rolling hill country. The Royal Palace is down on the sea-front, protected by the twin forts, Castel dell'Uovo and Castello Nuovo. On the hill above, over-looking the town, is the Royal Palace of Capodimonte, protected by the Castel di Sant'Elmo, and the town is spread between the two Palaces, rising on the steep sides of the hill, so that from almost every quarter of Naples one has a magnificent view of the curving bay, the sea and the islands. It is an ancient city, and in the late eighteenth century it was, after Paris, the largest city on the European continent. Stopendaal's mid-seventeenth-century map shows clearly the setting in which Emma arrived on her twenty-first birthday, 25 April 1786.

31

Red lacquer console table in the
Chinese taste, marble topped
height 33 $\frac{11}{16}$in (85·50cm)
depth 24⅝in (62·50cm)
width 51⅝in (131cm)
lent by the Museo di Capodimonte, Naples

The atmosphere in which Emma now found herself was one of greater glamour and affluence than she had left at Edgware Row. On 22 March 1787 Goethe described his reaction to Naples: 'The situation and the climate are beyond praise; but they are all the resources a foreigner has. Of course, someone with leisure, money and talent could settle down here and live most handsomely. This is what Sir William Hamilton has done in the evening of his days. The rooms in his villa, which he has furnished in the English taste, are charming and the view from the corner room may well be unique. The sea below, Capri opposite, Mount Posillipo to the right, nearby the promenade of the Villa Reale, to the left an old building of the Jesuits, in the distance the coast line from Sorrento to Cape Minerva – probably nothing comparable could be found in the whole of Europe and certainly not in the middle of a great city.' (Goethe, p. 207.)

In creating his well-furnished rooms Sir William got Italian craftsmen to build furniture to his own specifications. Neapolitan taste showed a marked preference for the curvilinear and the colourful: this table is a fine example of affluent Neapolitan furnishing.

| 32 | Table supported by caryatid sphinxes, mounted on goats' hoof feet, topped with gouache topographical drawings, under glass
height 32½in (82·50cm)
depth 19¹¹⁄₁₆in (50cm)
width 29⅛in (74cm)
lent by the Museo di Capodimonte, Naples |

PROV: Collezione Borboniche.

This table from the Neapolitan Royal Collection exemplifies the new Neoclassical taste in furniture which Sir William Hamilton did much to promote. He had local craftsmen copy details from antiques discovered at Pompeii and Herculaneum and, from these, original furnishings were made. The antique, and its recreation, was all the rage.

| 33 | Bibliothèque de Campagne, ou Amusemens de l'Esprit et du Coeur Vol. V
Amsterdam, Marc Michel Rey 1759
inscribed (on title page): *Catherine Hamilton 1759 . . . Emma Hamilton 1796*

lent by the National Maritime Museum, Greenwich |

In the first week of Emma's arrival in Naples in April 1786 she was able to report to Charles Greville: 'Sr. W. as given me a camels shawl like my old one. I know you will be pleased to hear that & he as given me a beautiful goun, cost 25 guineas, India painting on white sattin, & several little things of Lady Hamiltons & is going to by me some muslin dresses loose to tye with a sash for the hot weather, made like the turkey dresses, the sleeves tied in fowlds with ribban & trimmed with lace, in short he is all ways contriving what he shall get for me.' (Morrison, I, p. 150.) Although this volume is inscribed with Emma's married name, and dated ten years after her first arrival, it can perhaps be taken to represent the 'little things of Lady Hamiltons' which Sir William readily gave to her.

	Gavin Hamilton (1723–98)
34	Lady Hamilton as a Sibyl
Plate II	oil on canvas, 51 x 38in (129·5 x 96·5cm) in a plain gilded frame which bears an old inscription to Gavin Hamilton *lent by Mr and Mrs Clovis Whitfield*

PROV: Sir William Hamilton; sold 1801; recently from the collection of Sir Hamlyn Williams Drummond, Edwinsford, Carmarthenshire; deposited at the National Library of Wales, 1948; acquired by the present owners, 1972.

Emma, who had reconciled herself to departing for Naples on 1 March 1786, postponed the date – with relief one suspects – in order to have as an additional

travelling companion the Scottish painter, Gavin Hamilton. He was a man
admitted to be genial even by his detractors. Henry Fuseli in his expanded
edition of *Pilkington's Dictionary of Painters* (London, 1810), wrote 'however
eminent his talents or other qualities were, they were excelled by the liberality,
benevolence and humanity, of his character.' (Ibid., p. 226.) Since the 1750s
Gavin Hamilton had made his permanent residence in Italy, only occasionally
paying brief visits to Britain. In addition to painting, Gavin Hamilton pursued
archaeological interests. He had been to Naples, and must have found much in
common with Sir William Hamilton – they were both, in a sense, field archae-
ologists as well as collectors and both believed in excavation as the surest means
of discovering the finest antiquities. He was already 63 when he set out from
London in company with Emma and her mother. Although he left them at
Geneva on 27 March (Tours, p. 57), they must have renewed the acquaintance
within the year. Writing to Greville on 22 July 1786 Emma reported 'There
is two painters now in the house painting me; one picture is finished. It is the
size of the Bacante setting in a turbin, a turkish dress . . .' (Morrison, I, p. 117.)
One may surmise that Gavin Hamilton spent part of the summer of 1786 in
Naples painting Emma and this and Cat. No. 35 were the result. Gavin
Hamilton who only painted when he was definitely commissioned to do so,
may not have painted for many years longer: the last Royal Academy
Exhibition in which he showed a picture was 1788. Although it is not very
evident in his more famous classical subject pictures such as *Andromache Be-
wailing the Death of Hector* (1761), the present painting bears witness to the fact
that he valued the school of seventeenth-century Bologna most highly. For this
he was much despised by many of his contemporaries, including Henry Fuseli
who remarked 'Though solicitous about colour, he was no colourist; he should have
disdained what the grandeur of his subjects rejected, and content himself with
negative hues, and grave and simple tones, instead of the clammy greys, harsh
blues, and sordid reds, the refuse of the Roman and Bolognese schools, that cut
his breadth and dim his chiaroscuro.' (Op. cit., p. 226.) It was because of
opinions such as this that Gavin Hamilton's work has been so little known in
this country, and that two such beautiful portraits of Emma have only just
emerged from obscurity. Both these portraits may originally have formed part of
the collection of Sir William Hamilton. On 14 July 1798 Sir William made a
catalogue of his pictures hung in the Palazzo Sessa: in the room next to the
Library there were fifty-three pictures including two portraits of Emma, both
by Gavin Hamilton. (Catalogue of Sir William Hamilton's pictures, BM Add.
MSS. 41200, folios 121–6.) They were known as the Muses of Painting and
Poetry.

<table>
<tr><td></td><td>

Gavin Hamilton (1723–98)
Lady Hamilton as Hebe
oil on canvas, 50 x 37in (127 x 94cm)
in a plain gilded frame which bears an
old inscription to Gavin Hamilton
lent by Thomas Agnew & Sons
</td></tr>
<tr><td>

35
Plate III
</td><td></td></tr>
</table>

35
Plate III

Gavin Hamilton (1723–98)
Lady Hamilton as Hebe
oil on canvas, 50 x 37in (127 x 94cm)
in a plain gilded frame which bears an
old inscription to Gavin Hamilton
lent by Thomas Agnew & Sons

Another version in the collection of Lord Exeter at Burleigh House, was engraved
by Domenico Cunego, in Rome. It was shown in the exhibition *Angelika Kauffmann*

und ihre Zeitgenossen, Bregenz, July–October 1968; Vienna, November–February 1968–9, Cat. No. 274, as Gavin Hamilton after Angelica Kauffmann (no reasons given). It does not seem necessary to doubt the inscription on the present frame. The picture was probably painted in Naples in the summer of 1786. (See notes on Cat. No. 34.)

36

Filippo Tagliolini (?–1812)
Maria Carolina
Naples biscuit ware, Real Fabbrica
height 24 $\frac{13}{16}$ in (63cm)
depth 7 $\frac{7}{8}$ in (20cm)
lent by the Museo di Capodimonte, Naples

Royalty in Naples was less remote than in Great Britain; and Emma, although not acceptable at Court, must soon have become familiar with the appearance and public character of the King and Queen. Early in 1768 Maria Carolina of Austria, then aged 15, had been betrothed to the 17-year-old Ferdinand. It is said that when she was told the news she declared she might just as well be thrown into the sea. (Fothergill, p. 73.) By May she was married. Diplomats and visitors sent back numerous and often unflattering descriptions of the new Queen. (See Fothergill, p. 81.) Evidently she possessed little beauty even in her teens. But she was a powerful personality and perhaps most impartially and accurately weighed up by Hamilton's first wife, Catherine. Writing to a niece she said: 'I am no Courtier, and I know her Majesty's disposition too well to place any confidence in any encouragement she may be pleased to give me . . . She is quick, clever, insinuating when she pleases, hates and loves violently, but her passions of both kinds pass like the Wind; she is *too* proud and *too* humble, there is no dependence on what she says as she is seldom of the same opinion two days. Her strongest and most durable passions are ambition and vanity, the latter of which gives her a strong disposition to Coquetry, but the former, which I think is her principal Object, makes her use every Art to please the King in order to get the Reins of Government into her hands in as great a measure as is possible.' (E. and F. Anson: *Mary Hamilton*, London, 1925, p. 146.)

37

Caricature of Bernardo Tanucci
white porcelain, Real Fabbrica,
time of Ferdinando IV
height 4 $\frac{3}{4}$ in (12cm)
lent by the Museo di San Martino, Naples

PROV: Marcello Orilia, Naples; acquired by the Museo di San Martino 1953.
EXH: *Mostra del Ritratto Storico Napoletano*, Naples, 1954, p. 86; *Il Risorgimento in Terra di Lavoro*, Caserta, 1961, p. 53.

An instance of the license given by Neapolitan royalty to irreverence for authority, this superb but cruel caricature of the Marquis Tanucci, chief Minister of the Kingdom of the two Sicilies during the minority of Ferdinando IV, was produced in the Royal porcelain factory. In Naples political success was no guarantee of popularity. Celebrity tended to be of the kind represented by this caricature – even although Tanucci was, according to Hamilton, the only member of the Regency not bent on lining his own pockets. (Letter to the Secretary of State,

BM Egerton MSS. 2634, fo. 192, quoted by Fothergill, p. 50.) Tanucci was loathed by Maria Carolina. Within two years of her gaining a seat on the Council of State in 1775, he was dismissed from office – surely an appropriate moment for the appearance of a caricature?

Pietro Fabris (flourished in Naples 2nd half of the eighteenth century)
Peasants feasting with a view of the Bay of Naples
oil on canvas,
29¾ x 59¾in (75·5 x 151·8cm)
lent anonymously

38

Pietro Fabris, an artist of Italian extraction, was a British subject who spent most of his life in Naples. He was an old acquaintance of Sir William Hamilton's, having worked under his close supervision when making the plates for Hamilton's magnificent *Campi Phlegraei, Observations on the Volcanoes of the Two Sicilies,* published in three volumes, 1776–9. So successful were these plates that it is no wonder that Hamilton kept in touch with the artist, and remained one of his patrons. When Lord Gardenstone visited the Palazzo Sessa some time after Emma's arrival he recorded seeing a painting by Fabris which represented 'in a very pleasing stile the characters and humours of the people of Naples'. (*Travelling Memorandums made in a Tour upon the Continent of Europe,* Vol. III, p. 98 – quoted by Fothergill, pp. 115–16.) *Peasants feasting with a view of the Bay of Naples* is just such a subject, and although we have no reason to believe that it ever actually belonged to Sir William Hamilton, we may take it as typical both of the work of Fabris which Emma must have found at the Palazzo Sessa on her arrival, and of the Neapolitan contemporary scene.

The view is from Posillipo where Sir William had had, since the days of his first wife, a small villa. This he renamed the 'Villa Emma', and it is still known as that today. In 1779 it was described by Lord Herbert as 'the last house a carriage can arrive at'. (*Pembroke Papers,* Vol. I, p. 225; quoted by Fothergill p. 61.) Its seclusion did not deter Sir William, and he and Emma spent much time there in the hot summer months. Sir William improved upon the scene: from a letter written by Tischbein to Goethe on 10 July 1787 we learn of one of his favourite diversions at Posillipo. 'The day before yesterday I visited Sir William Hamilton in his Posillipo villa. There is really no more glorious place in the whole world. After lunch a dozen boys went swimming in the sea. It was beautiful to watch the groups they made, and the postures they took during their games. Sir William pays them to give him this pleasure.' (Goethe, p. 349.) This is the only instance we know of Sir William's providing guests with an after luncheon entertainment different from, but comparable to Emma's famous 'Attitudes'. The little villa, which itself became a grandstand for this entertainment, was described by Lord Herbert in his diary: 'It is built on a small rock, and consists of three rooms and a kitchen with a very diminutive garden. There are two flights of stairs to come up to it. When the weather is fine a small terrass before the building constitutes the Setting Room with a large Venetian blind over it to guard it from the heat of the sun.'

39

Philip Hackert (1737–1807)
Harvest time at Carditello:
Ferdinando IV and his family in
peasant costume
oil on canvas, 21¼ x 40 15/16 in (54 x 104cm)
lent by the Museo di San Martino, Naples

PROV: from the Palace of Capodimonte.
LIT: N. Spinosa; *La pittura Napoletana da Carla a Ferdinando IV di Borbone*, Naples, 1971; Goethe, pl. 25. (As by C. H. Kniep.)
One of a pair, the other being *I Figli di Ferdinando IV alle Vendemmia da Contadini*, this was formerly attributed to C. H. Kniep: from the evidence of existing drawings they are now ascribed by R. Causa and N. Spinosa to Philip Hackert.

Although Emma on her first arrival was not in a position to attend the court at Naples, she did frequently see the King, Ferdinando IV, who was a rollicking monarch with a love for low company. Fears that he might be afflicted with congenital madness like his late grandfather, Philip V of Spain in old age, or his late uncle Ferdinand VI of Spain, or indeed his own elder brother Don Philip, had prompted his tutors to avoid intellectual instruction almost entirely. Apart from field sports of the day, he had been given practically no instruction in any subject whatever. His bucolic existence was sometimes seconded by Queen Maria Carolina who, like her sister Marie Antoinette of France, affected from time to time the romantic simplicity of peasant life. Here for instance she and her large family are shown indulging in the fantasy that they are helping to harvest the crops. In Naples such play-acting brought the royal family far closer to the people than it did in France. Emma cannot have felt that royalty was very aloof.

Philip Hackert was a topographical painter who had left his native Germany to work in Naples and Sicily. He had won the regard and even friendship of both Ferdinand and Maria Carolina who had consequently made him their official court painter. Goethe visiting Naples in February 1787, inspected Hackert's studio in the wing of the old palace of Francavilla which had been reserved for his sole use. Hackert was a man who could frequent easily all levels of society. Goethe commented: 'Though Hackert is always busy drawing and painting, he remains sociable and has a gift for attracting people and making them become his pupils.' (Goethe, p. 197.) Emma took drawing lessons, possibly from Hackert. Goethe saw at once that Hackert's position at Court was of great importance to the interests of art in Naples: 'The fact that he is not only giving drawing lessons to the Princesses, but is also called upon in the evening to give lectures on art and other related subjects is evidence of the special trust with which the Queen honours him.'

40

Large bowl and saucer, en suite,
decorated with Pompeian
dancers
porcelain, Real Fabbrica
bowl height 3 15/16 in (10cm)
plate diameter 8⅝in (21·9cm)
mark on both saucer and bowl an 'N'

40 cont.

surmounted by a crown; blue
lent by the Comune di Napoli (Museo Floridiana)

PROV: Duca di Martina collection.
EXH: *Il settecento Italiano,* Venice, 1929.
LIT: E. Romano, 'La Porcellana di Capodimonte' AFSG. 16052.

This and the following three items are decorated with dancing figures copied from Pompeian frescoes. Both the originals and the many reproductions of them must have become familiar to Emma early in her Neapolitan experience.

Naples in the eighteenth century was a great centre of the ceramic industry. Local taste favoured porcelain painted either with topographical scenes or else with brilliant lively designs in vivid colours. While there was no hesitation to paint fine Sèvres with a still life of vegetables, the motifs most popular with the cognoscenti and visiting antiquarians alike, about the time of Emma's arrival in Naples were reproductions of the twelve small dancing figures found on fresco decorations at Pompeii. Eight of these had been found in the house tentatively identified as that of Crassus Frugius. The excavations of the house date from 1749–78, and the dancers were found at the beginning of that period, their discovery being reported by the Spanish archaeologist R. I. d'Alcubierre, in the course of work carried out on 15 and 18 January 1749. (*Rapport des excavations de la Civita* cited by Charles Bonucci, *Pompei décrite*, Naples, 1830, p. 251.) These antique dancers became important not only to the painters of porcelain, but to Emma Hart. On 27 May 1787 Goethe reported to J. G. Herder a curious discovery made the previous evening in the basement of the Palazzo Sessa: 'I was greatly intrigued by a chest which was standing upright. Its front had been taken off, the interior painted black and the whole set inside a splendid gilt frame. It was large enough to hold a standing human figure, and that, we were told, was exactly what it was meant for. Not content with seeing his image of beauty as a moving statue, this friend of art and girlhood wished also to enjoy her as an inimitable painting, and so, standing against this black background in dresses of various colours, she had sometimes imitated the paintings of Pompeii or even more recent masterpieces. This phase, it seems, is now over, because it was difficult to transport the apparatus and light it properly, and so we were not to share in this spectacle.' (Goethe, p. 311.) Emma had early reported to Greville a visit to Pompeii (letter 22 July 1786, Morrison, I, p. 117) and evidently this first experiment at a *tableau vivant* was among her earliest efforts at drawing-room entertainment in Naples. What is uncertain is whether it was a variation devised to suit the context, or the first experiment in a series of dumb shows which were to develop into her celebrated 'Attitudes'. There, is only one extant letter in which she mentions performing the Attitudes: the immensely long one which she wrote to Greville between August and December 1787. Towards the end of it, having spoken of the terror of the people at the renewed eruptions of Vesuvius she continues complacently: 'And, Greville, its true that the have all got it in their heads I am like the Virgin, and the do come to beg favours of me. Last night their was two priests came to our house, and Sir William made me put the shawl over my head, and look up, and the priest burst into tears and kist my feet and said, "God had sent me a purpose." O, à propo! Now as I have such a use of shawls, and mine is wore out, Sir William is miserable, for I stand in attitudes with them on me. As you know Mr Mack Pherson, ask him to give you one for me. Pray do, for mine is wore out.' (Morrison, I, p. 133.) The use of a shawl, necessarily rather limited within the box, was extensive only in the vivid dramatic depiction of action which constituted the later more famous Attitudes. (See Cat. Nos. 44 and 45.) Of the twelve Attitudes originally published Nos. VI and VIII are most obviously inspired by the same Pompeian dancers to be seen on this porcelain.

41

Pair of Sèvres vases decorated in Naples with Pompeian dancers
porcelain, Sèvres
height 11 $\frac{13}{16}$ in (30cm)
width 4 $\frac{3}{4}$ in (12cm)
lent by the Museo di Capodimonte, Naples

See notes on Cat. No. 40.

42

Vase decorated with Bacchante in green and mauve, with censer
porcelain, Real Fabbrica
height 19 $\frac{11}{16}$ in (50cm)
width 9 $\frac{7}{8}$ in (25cm)
lent by the Museo di Capodimonte, Naples

See notes on Cat. No. 40.

43

Milk jug decorated with Pompeian dancers and black and white bands *c.* 1795–1800
porcelain, Real Fabbrica
height 4 $\frac{5}{16}$ in (11cm)
width 2 $\frac{9}{16}$ in (6·5cm)
depth 3 $\frac{5}{16}$ in (8·5cm)
lent by the Museo Correale di Terranova, Sorrento

See notes on Cat. No. 40.

Frederick Rehberg

44

Drawings faithfully copied from Nature at Naples and with permission dedicated to the Right Honourable Sir William Hamilton, His Britanic Majesty's Envoy Extraordinary and Plenipotentiary at the Court of Naples. By his most humble Servant Frederick Rehberg, Historical Painter in his Prussian Majesty's Service at

Rome . . . Engrav'd by Thomas Piroli
Rome, Niccola de Antonj, n.d.
folio, thirteen leaves engraved throughout. Mid nineteenth-century binding,
marbled boards, $\frac{1}{2}$ calf. The leaves, now
mounted and stitched at the spine, were
previously stab-stitched, presumably
when issued
$15\frac{1}{3}$ x 11in (39·3 x 28cm)
lent anonymously

These are the original twelve plates and title page engraved by Thomas Piroli after drawings by Frederick Rehberg. So far no date has been established for the drawings or for the first publication of the prints. Another set of twenty-four plates, including slavish copies of this original set, was published in 1794. (See Cat. No. 45.) Apparently simultaneously these twelve plates were reissued, presumably in Rome, the printer's name being erased on the title page and the date inserted. (See Holmström, fig. 45.) Mrs Gram Holmström takes the dated issue to be the first edition (op. cit., p. 119), but it must have been preceded by the present issue, for the printer's name gives no indication of having been inserted over cancellations. The title page is decorated with a portrait of Emma in a roundel initialled 'E.H.', but this provides no clue, as her initials remained the same before and after marriage. Although the dedication is to Sir William Hamilton, Emma's name is nowhere mentioned. Surely the drawings must have been produced in the early years of their intimacy, before her marriage? The publication of a set of prints is a very different matter from the production of portraits for private collections. As can be seen from the evidence cited by Mrs Gram Holmström, such sets of prints demonstrating dramatic action or psychological interpretation were always associated with the theatre or actresses – an association which might seem of no detrimental consequence in the case of young Mrs Hart, protegée of Sir William Hamilton, but one singularly inappropriate for the wife of the British Envoy Plenipotentiary at the Court of Naples, especially when that lady was trying to live down a dubious past. Once issued, the prints had become public property and were frequently repeated: a German edition came out post 1794 engraved by Schenck, with introduction and legends in French and German. (See Holmström, p. 119.) It was probably a case of Sir William's being unable to check the reissue of plates he had himself published before any notion of marriage was forced into his life – possibly in 1788.

The actual performance of Attitudes must have been very frequent if her shawl was already worn out by December 1787 (see Cat. No. 40) – moreover, Sir William Hamilton had given her a new camel shawl soon after her arrival. (See notes to Cat. No. 33.) Mrs Gram Holmström's thesis contains the most authoritative survey of Emma's Attitudes to date: 'It was in Romney's studio that Emma Hart learnt to pose, to control and develop her talent for mimoplastic expression and to handle draperies in the antique style. . . . It is note-worthy that this mimoplastic art is not an emanation from the contemporary English theatre.' (Op. cit., 135–6.) The first part of this statement is wholly acceptable; but the second should be modified. Romney was passionately interested in the theatre (William Hayley, *Memoirs of the Life and Writings of William Hayley*, London, H. Colburn & Co., 1823, I, pp. 287–9); and at the time that Emma sat to him most frequently, he was in particularly close contact with the brilliant exponent of naturalism, John Henderson. (See notes on Cat. No. 3.) Henderson and Romney, with six others including Sheridan senior and Evans the bookseller, belonged to a club, the Unincreasibles, devoted to theatrical interests. (John Romney, p. 167.) Emma probably practised modelling in a professional sense in Romney's studio. She must have taken up poses and held them for a protracted period while Romney painted.

Posing within the box (see notes on Cat. No. 40) would have been a natural refinement of such static modelling. The idea of depicting a developing action may have been Sir William Hamilton's – it was he who instructed her how to pose for the priests. (See notes on Cat. No. 40.) It was a totally new art form, and Emma had certainly developed a high degree of professional skill in performing her Attitudes by the time that Goethe gave his famous account of them. Writing on 16 March 1787 he reported, 'it is a strange experience for me to be in a society where everyone does nothing but enjoy himself. Sir William Hamilton, who is still living here as English ambassador, has now, after many years of devotion to the arts and the study of nature, found the acme of these delights in the person of an English girl of 20 with a beautiful face and a perfect figure. He has had a Greek costume made for her which becomes her extremely. Dressed in this, she lets down her hair and, with a few shawls gives so much variety to her poses, gestures, expressions, etc., that the spectator can hardly believe his eyes. He sees what thousands of artists would have liked to express realised before him in movements and surprising transformations – standing, kneeling, sitting, reclining, serious, sad, playful, ecstatic, contrite, alluring, threatening, anxious, one pose follows another without a break. She knows how to arrange the folds of her veil to match each mood, and has a hundred ways of turning it into a headdress. The old knight idolises her and is enthusiastic about everything she does. In her he has found all the antiquities, all the profiles of Sicilian coins, even the Apollo Belvedere. This much is certain: as a performance it's like nothing you ever saw before in your life. We have already enjoyed it on two evenings.' (Goethe, pp. 199–200.)

For many Emma had a charm in the Attitudes which she possessed at no other moment. After a slight acquaintance of two months the sensitive Goethe was in many ways disenchanted. On 27 May he wrote 'I must confess that our fair entertainer seems to me, frankly, a dull creature. Perhaps her figure makes up for it, but her voice is inexpressive and her speech without charm. Even her singing is neither full-throated nor agreeable.' (Goethe, p. 312.) It was not merely Goethe's ignorance of English that made him prefer Emma silent. Lady Holland found the accent and the lack of refinement too much: 'Just as she was lying down, with her head reclining upon an Etruscan vase to represent a water-nymph, she exclaimed in her provincial dialect: "Doun't be afeared Sir Willum, I'll not crack your *joug*." I turned away disgusted. . . .' (Earl of Ilchester (ed.) *Journal of Elizabeth, Lady Holland*, London, 1908, I, p. 243.) For a fuller contemporary description of the Attitudes see *Mémoires de la Comtesse de Boigne*, ed. M. Charles Nicoullaud, I (1781–1814), Paris, 1907, pp. 114 ff.

The Attitudes did earn for her some unkind epithets: Horace Walpole referred to 'Sir William Hamilton's Pantomime Mistress', and after the marriage he wrote to Miss Berry 'Sir William has actually married his Gallery of Statues'.

45

Frederick Rehberg and others
Drawings Faithfully copied from Nature . . . MDCCXCIV
[N.p., no engraver's name]
inscribed: (on frontispiece)
'*Outlines of Figures and Drapery*
Collected with great care from Antient
Statues, Monuments Basreleivos &c
representing the principle Characters in the
Plays of Racine, in their proper Costume
forming an useful Study for Amateurs in
Drawing, from the most correct & chaste
Models of Grecian & Roman Sculpture.'
title-page, frontispiece and twenty-four plates etched throughout
nineteenth-century cloth binding, bland-stamped and lettered in gold on front: *Lady Hamilton's Attitudes.*
lent anonymously

The title page and the last twelve plates are slavish copies of the plates in Cat. No. 44. The additional sources from which this new collection was drawn are indicated on the frontispiece. A woman sits drawing from 'Fores's Correct Costume of Several Nations of Antiquity' while at her feet lie three more collections of plates inscribed 'Lady Hamilton's Attitudes', 'Metz's Drawing Book' and 'Heads for studies'. As six out of the additional twelve plates show males, it has always been assumed that Emma included male impersonations in her 'Attitudes', the other sources indicated on the frontispiece being ignored.

46

A female figure
Naples biscuit ware, Real Fabbrica
height 10 $\frac{13}{16}$ in (27·50cm)
lent by the Museo de Capodimonte, Naples

PROV: from the De Ciccio Collection, No. 512.
During the reign of Ferdinando IV depiction of classical poses was not confined to paintings on porcelain. In Naples, so close to Pompeii and Herculaneum, it was almost an industry. Emma in devising her Attitudes had many models to choose from. This and Cat. Nos. 47, 48 and 49 are examples of the many ceramic figures inspired by the antique.

47

Clio
Naples biscuit ware, Real Fabbrica
height 8 $\frac{7}{16}$ in (21·5cm)
width 1 $\frac{3}{4}$ in (4·5cm)
depth 4 $\frac{3}{4}$ in (12cm)

47 cont.   *lent by the Museo Correale di Terranova,*
                                               Sorrento

See notes on Cat. No. 46.
This represents Clio, the Muse of History, in her conventional antique pose.

48   Peace
                                               earthenware in white majolica,
                                               Manifattura Giustiniani, Naples
                                               height 11in (28cm)
                                               lent by the Museo di Capodimonte, Naples
PROV: from the De Ciccio Collection, No. 498.
See notes on Cat. No. 46.

49   A female figure
                                               earthenware in white majolica,
                                               Manifattura Giustiniani, Naples
                                               height 11in (28cm)
                                               lent by the Museo di Capodimonte, Naples
PROV: from the De Ciccio Collection, No. 449.
See notes on Cat. No. 46.

                                               Madame Louise-Elisabeth
                                               Vigée-Le Brun (1755–1842)
50   Emma as a Bacchante
                                               oil on canvas,
                                               53 x 62in (134·6 x 157·5cm)
                                               signed: (lower l.) *Vigée-Le Brun*
                                               inscribed: *Napoli*
                                               lent anonymously
PROV: Sir William Hamilton; sold Christie's 1801; Admiral Sir Horatio Nelson;
among the contents of Merton bequeathed to Lady Hamilton; sold by her to
pay debts; bought by Tankerville Chamberlayne.
LIT: *Souvenirs de Madame Louise-Elisabeth Vigée-Le Brun*, 3 vols., Paris 1835–7,
II, pp. 86–8; Baily, pl. facing p. 24.
Mme Vigée-Le Brun's memoirs, published in old age, show such a malicious
dislike to Emma that modern apologists for Lady Hamilton have dismissed
her evidence as unreliable. However, the portraits she made of Emma belong to
an earlier and happier period in their relationship. Madame Vigée-Le Brun
came to Naples, as did many other French Royalists, in 1789, driven from Paris
by the disturbances of the Revolution. Her social sphere was soon centred on the
Russian Embassy, and the Ambassador, whom she refers to as 'Le comté de
Scawronnki', demanded that she paint his wife before anyone else. She had
just begun this portrait when 'je vis arriver chez moi le chavalier Hamilton,
ambassadeur d'Angleterre à Naples, qui me demandait en grâce que mon
premier portrait fût celui d'une superbe femme qu'il me présenta; c'était
madame Hart, sa maîtresse . . . Je peignis madame Hart couchée au bord de la
mer, tenant une coupe à la main. Sa belle figure était fort animée et contrastait
complètement avec celle de la comtesse; elle avait une quantité énorme de

beaux cheveux châtains qui pouvaient la couvrir entièrement, et en bacchante, ses cheveux épars, elle était admirable.' (Op. cit., II, pp. 86–7.)

Sir William, financially embarrassed after his return to England, sold this portrait in 1801 along with other paintings formerly in the Palazzo Sessa. Madame Le Brun complained bitterly that he got 300gns for it although when she painted it he drove such a hard bargain that he only gave her 90gns. (Ibid., p. 88.) Nelson was incensed at Hamilton's parting with the picture, and wrote to Emma on 11 March 1801: 'I see clearly, my dearest friend, you are on SALE.' (Morrison, II, p. 128.) By July 1802 he had bought the painting himself – as we know from a letter of William Hamilton's to Henry Bone the miniaturist. Bone was commissioned by Sir William to make a miniature after the painting, and this miniature he eventually left to Nelson in a codicil to his will. (Morrison, II, p. 424.) It is now in the Wallace Collection. (See W. P. Gibson, *Wallace Collection . . . Miniatures and Illuminations*, 1935, M. 21, pp. 11–12.) The painting must have been Nelson's favourite among the fourteen portraits of Emma which hung in the Palazzo Sessa when Hamilton made the catalogue of his pictures on 14 July 1798. (Fothergill, p. 299.) In the codicil to his Will Sir William wrote: 'The copy of Madam Le Brunn's picture of Emma in enamel, by Bone, I give to my dearest friend Lord Nelson Duke of Bronte, a very small token of the great regard I have for his Lordship, the most virtuous, loyal, and truly brave character I ever met with. God bless him, and shame fall on those who do not say amen.' Twenty-three days later Sir William Hamilton died.

Ambition to become Lady Hamilton

Emma had been in Naples less than three years when Sir William began to realise, with apprehension, that her greatest ambition was to become Lady Hamilton. One cannot help sympathising with Emma, not only because Sir William was so obviously an extremely charming companion. Only three months after she had first arrived in Naples she wrote forlornly to Greville whom she still hoped to win back 'I have a language master, a singing master, musick, etc., etc., but what is it for, if it was to amuse you I should be happy, but Greville, what shall it avail me. I am poor, helpless & forlorn. I have lived with you 5 years & you have sent me to a strange place & no one prospect, me thinking you was coming to me; instead of which I was told I was to live, you know how, with Sir W. No. I respect him, but no, never shall he perhaps live with me for a little wile like you & send me to England, then what am I to do, what is to become of me.' (22 July 1786. Morrison, I, p. 117.)

The fascination of the story arises from our being able to sympathise as deeply with Sir William as with Emma. As early as August 1786 Emma had warned Greville: 'If you affront me, I will make him marry me.' (1 August 1786. Morrison, I, p. 119.)

When in 1790 rumours were circulating that Hamilton and Emma were already secretly married, Sir William had to reply to his old friend Sir Joseph Banks who had written a letter of inquiry. 'To answer your question fairly, was I in a private station I should have no objection that Emma should share with me *le petit bout de vie qui me reste* under the solemn covenant you allude to, as her behaviour in my house has been such for four years as to gain her universal esteem and approbation, but as I have no thoughts of relinquishing my Employment and whilst I am in a public character, I do not look upon myself at liberty to act as I please, and such a step I think wou'd be imprudent and might be attended with disagreeable circumstances – besides, as amidst other branches of natural History I have not neglected the study of the animal called Woman, I have found them subject to great changes according to circumstances and I do not like to try experiments at my time of life.' (6 April 1790, BM Add. MSS. 34048 fo. 61.) Sir William was in a difficult position. He owed the happy life he enjoyed to having inherited property from his first wife, and to having held, since 1764, his position in Naples as Minister of the British Crown. To marry Emma was to be disloyal to both those benefactors. Moreover, Sir William was by now nearly 60 and Emma only 25. He was, however, an idealist, and he felt strongly about the injustice which was blighting Emma's life. From remarks in this very same letter Banks must have suspected what the outcome would be. 'I assure you' wrote Sir William frankly 'that I approve of her so much that if I had been the person that made her first go astray, I wou'd glory in giving her a public reparation, and I would do it openly, for indeed she has infinite merit and no Princess cou'd do the honours of her Palace with more care and dignity than she does those of my house; in short she is worthy of anything, and I have and will take care of her in proportion as I feel myself oblighed to her.' They are sentiments which Nelson was to echo not so many years later – amazement that anybody, ever, could have jilted Emma. Sir William adored her, but he married her to right an injustice he had not initiated and would not have sanctioned. How much his decision was affected by the turmoil of Europe at the collapse of the old Regime, and the pessimistic feeling that the old order was changing irrevocably, is matter for speculation. The fervour of war was mounting in Europe when they left Naples for England in 1791.

51

Dominique Vivant De Non
(1747-1825)
Madame Hart 1791
etching by Jean Suntach
trimmed to plate marks,
8⅜ x 5⅜in (21·3 x 13·6cm)
inscribed: (etched in plate) *Madame*
Hart . . . 1791 . . . Dessinée par M. De
Non . . . Gravée par M. Jean Suntach

lent anonymously

LIT: Baily, p. 126.

A rare etched portrait of Emma, presumably made in Naples in the early months of 1791. In April that year she, with her mother and Sir William, set out on the journey to England where she was, at last, to marry and become Lady Hamilton.

52

? C. Newings
L'Allegro and Il Penseroso
a pair of watercolour drawings
each approximately
9¾ x 7⅜in (24·8 x 18·7cm)
Il Penseroso inscribed (lower l):
C. Newings

lent anonymously

Such was Sir William Hamilton's success as a patron of the arts and a promoter of Emma's finer qualities that when she returned to England with him in May 1791 she was welcomed as a reigning beauty. Only lesser artists made such drawings as these, which might be interpreted as caricatures of her Attitudes. They were acquired for a collection rich in portraits of Emma.

53
Plate v

George Romney (1734–1802)
Lady Hamilton as The Ambassadress 1791
oil on canvas,
50 x 39½in (127 x 100·3cm)
lent by Mr and Mrs Jack G. Taylor,
Austin, Texas

PROV: In the possession of George Romney until 13 December 1800, when it was delivered to Mrs Cadogan, mother of Lady Hamilton; Sir Robert Bateson Harvey; Sir Robert Grenville Harvey, Langley Park, Bucks.; Baron Herbert de Stern, first Lord Michelham; Sale Hampton & Sons, London, 24 November 1926, lot 294; Duveen Brothers, New York; the Hon Jack Herbert Michelham, London.

EXH: *Woman and Child in Art*, Grosvenor Gallery, London, November 1913, No. 26; *Forty British Portraits*; Duveen Brothers, New York, 9–30 April, 1940, No. 40.

LIT: Ward and Roberts, II, p. 186, No. 30 (called *With Vesuvius in the Distance*); Hilda Gamlin, *George Romney and his art*, London, Swan Sonnenschein & Co., 1894, p. 177; Chamberlain, p. 167; Baily, *Repr.* facing p. 40 (called *Lady Hamilton as the Ambassadress*); in *The Art Digest*, 1 December 1926, I, p. 12; in *Century Cyclopedia of Names*, c. 1911, p. 477; in *Burlington Magazine*, November 1926, XLIII, p. xliii; Millia Davenport, *The Book of Costumes*, New York, 1948, II, p. 787, No. 2221; engraved in mezzotint by T. G. Appleton, 1905.

Emma's return to England in May 1791 caused great excitement in the art world, and not least to George Romney. It was a moment when Romney was particularly depressed. With Hayley he had visited Paris in the summer of 1790. His political sympathies were anti-Royalist, and he had been thrown into a state of ferment by witnessing the progress of Revolutionary activities. Since the return from France his health had not been good, and his work had been hampered by the absence of his assistant, visiting his sick father in the country (there is a draft letter to the assistant in a sketch-book inscribed 'Spring 1791' sold at Sotheby's, 14 November 1962, lot 51). On 3 May he wrote to Hayley 'my mind is labouring under some anxiety, and depression of spirits, which has indeed been the case with me for some time past'. (Hayley, p. 156.) However, on 22 May he wrote again in a quite different mood. (See Hayley's list of Romney's letters to him, BM Add. MSS. 30805.) Hayley summarised the letter: 'The fair Emma . . . surprised him by an early visit one morning in a Turkish habit, and attended by Sir William Hamilton.' Emma was wearing, and popularising in London, the original classical style in which Sir William had dressed her on her first arrival in Naples. (See notes on Cat. No. 33.) Romney was ecstatic. Her name appear in his Sitters' Diaries for 2, 4, 8, 11, 14, 17, 19, 20, 22, 23, 25, 27, 29 June, 1, 2, 3, 4, 6, 7, 9, 10, 11, 14, 16, 18, 19, 20 July, 22, 23, 26 August, 4, 5, 6 September. The last two of these entries are the famous ones which read 'Mrs Hart at 9' and 'Lady Hamilton at 11'. It appears Emma never sat to him again. He had put off having a holiday all summer long mainly on her account (Hayley, p. 158) and so it is not entirely surprising that after her marriage there should be a diary gap of over five weeks. An indication that his illness and depression had returned may be seen in the fact that for the remainder of the year he almost invariably accepted only one sitter each day.

Among the subjects he worked on in 1791 using **Emma as model** were *Joan of Arc*, a *Magdalen*, a *Bacchante* and a companion piece (both for the Prince of Wales) and a picture of *Constance* for the Shakespeare Gallery. He valued her good sense as highly as her beauty and reported to Hayley 'all the world following her and talking of her, so that if she had not more good sense, than vanity, her brain must be turned'. (See letter dated 17 July 1791, quoted by Hayley, p. 159.) Not only did artists clamour loudly to paint her (see Cat. No. 57) but society was enthusiastic about her singing and acting. Again Romney reported to Hayley on 8 August 'In my last letter I think I informed you, that I was going to dine with Sir William and his Lady. In the evening of that day, there were collected several people of fashion to hear her sing. She performed, both in the serious and comic, to admiration, both in singing and acting; but her Nina surpasses everything I ever saw, and I believe, as a piece of acting, nothing ever surpassed it. The whole company were in an agony of sorrow. Her acting is simple, grand, terrible and pathetic. My mind was so much heated, that I was for running down to Eartham to fetch you up to see her.' (Hayley, pp. 161–2.)

The present picture, *The Ambassadress*, is the most important portrait Romney painted of Emma at this period, and probably the most formal one he ever made of her. It has been suggested that she is shown in her wedding dress. She sits on a sofa leaning on the arm and turns her head towards the spectator, as if just interrupted at prayer. In the background can be seen Vesuvius. It is a portrait redolent with respectability, and eventually became the property of her mother.

George Romney (1734–1802)
Lady Hamilton as a Bacchante with a Vase

54

oil on canvas, 50 x 40in (127 x 101·6cm)
lent by the Norton Simon Foundation,
Los Angeles, California

PROV: Sir John Fleming Leicester, Bt, 1st Lord de Tabley; Sir George Warren Leicester; Lady Eleanor Leighton; Cuthbert Leicester Warren, Esq., JP, High Sheriff of Cheshire, Tabley House, Knutsford; sold Christie's 20 May 1927, lot 38, *Repr.*; Duveen Brothers Inc, New York; the Norton Simon Foundation, Los Angeles.

EXH: *Art Treasures*, Manchester 1857, No. 631; British Institution, London, 1863, No. 116; *Old Masters*, Royal Academy 1884, No. 211; Galerie Charpentier, Paris, 1934; *Les Anglais sur la Riviera*, Musée Massena, Nice, 1934, No. 349; *Forty British Portraits*, Duveen Brothers Inc, New York, 1940, No. 39; on loan to the Worcester Art Museum, 1965–71.

LIT: William Carey, *Descriptive Catalogue of the Works of Art in the Collection of Sir John Fleming Leicester, Bart.*, 1810, p. 129; John Young, *Catalogue of Pictures by British Artists in the possession of Sir John Fleming Leicester, Bart., at Tabley House, Cheshire*, London, 1821, p. 30, No. 66, *Repr.* (etching); Ward and Roberts, II, p. 181, No. 3k; Julia Frankau, *The Story of Emma, Lady Hamilton*, London, 1911, II, p. 95; Algernon Graves, *A Century of Loan Exhibitions*, London, 1914, III, p. 1114; A. Avray Tipping in *English Homes* (Period IV), London, I, p. 42 'Tabley House, Cheshire'; *Art News*, April 23, 1927, *Repr.*; *Art News*, April 30, 1927, p. 2; Margaret Miller in *Apollo*, June 1940, pp. 166–7; Helen Comstock in *Connoisseur*, July 1940, pp. 28–9; Sidney Tillim in *Arts*, November 1960, p. 57; Mark Roskill in *Art News*, November 1960, p. 13.

Many of Romney's most famous portraits of Emma show her as a Bacchante. (See notes to Cat. Nos. 9, 10 and 11.) This is a little known version, the head alone having the appearance of being painted from the living model. The landscape setting at the edge of a wood is particularly attractive. As the pose has much in common with the Fuseliesque versions of Queen Mab which Romney was painting in 1791 (see Folger Shakespeare Library sketch book inscribed 'Queen Mab') it may be a painting begun in that year.

Henry Fuseli (1741–1825)
Sketch of Emma

55

pencil, 9 x 7½in (22·9 x 19cm)

inscribed: *Lady Hamilton July 1–17*
lent by D. L. T. Oppé, Esq

PROV: A. P. Oppé; bequeathed to the present owner.

The inscription on this sheet is puzzling, if one is to assume that it is in the artist's autograph, and the drawing made, as one would suppose, in 1791. Emma was not married until 6 September that year, and therefore could not properly have been referred to as 'Lady Hamilton' in July. There is no reason to doubt that the sketch was made by Fuseli and does represent Emma on some informal occasion, although it has not hitherto been recorded that he ever took her likeness.

56

Joseph Nollekens (1737–1823)
Emma Hart in a tragic rôle
white marble
height 22 $\frac{15}{16}$ in (58·3cm) – with base,
base 4$\frac{1}{4}$in (10·8cm)
width 15$\frac{5}{8}$in (39·7cm)
depth 9$\frac{5}{8}$in (24·4cm)
signed: (on reverse) *Nollekens Ft.*
lent by the Visitors of the Ashmolean
Museum, Oxford

PROV: Alfred Spero; Major W. W. Dowding; Sale Christie's 21 January 1965, lot 11; purchased by the Ashmolean Museum, 1965, Bouch Bequest Fund.
LIT: Report of the Visitors, Ashmolean Museum, Oxford, 1965, pp. 56–7, *Repr.* pl. XI.

Joseph Nollekens may have been one of the other artists to whom Emma sat in 1791. The date of the present bust is uncertain. Nollekens was by nature an intensely secretive man, and a miser. Like Gavin Hamilton, however, he was passionately interested in antique works of art, particularly sculpture. He frequently restored damaged antiques working extensively, for instance, on the Townley marbles. Like Sir William Hamilton he often dealt in antique works of art; and he sometimes went into partnership with Gavin Hamilton to do so. (See John Thomas Smith, *Nollekens and his Times* edited by Wilfred Witten, two vols., 1920, I, pp. 12, 155–6, 207, 208.) Nollekens moved in the same circles not only as Gavin Hamilton, but also as Charles Greville. (Op. cit., I, p. 214.) It is quite easy to account for Emma's having sat to Nollekens, but more difficult to fix a precise date. This bust may have been made in the summer of 1791. In it Nollekens (or perhaps Emma in the pose she adopted) seems to draw upon knowledge of the Medici Niobe. In a sketch book which came to the Ashmolean as part of the Douce Bequest in 1834 are to be found drawings of the Medici Niobe. These, on the strength of comparison with inscribed and dated drawings by Nollekens of the Medici Venus (also in the Ashmolean Museum), are dated to 1770. (Information on the drawings kindly supplied by the Ashmolean Museum.)

57

Sir Thomas Lawrence (1769–1830)
Head of Emma 1791
pencil,

57 cont.
oval: $7\frac{7}{8}$ x 6in (20 x 15·2cm)
inscribed: (lower l in ink) *Emma 1791*
lent by the Trustees of the British Museum

PROV: Given to the British Museum by Payne Knight. (BM No. Payne Knight Oo. 5–22.)

LIT: Lord Ronald Sutherland Gower: *Lawrence*, London, 1900, *Repr.* p. 65; Laurence Binyon: *Catalogue of Drawings by British Artists and Artists of Foreign Origin working in Great Britain*, London, Trustees of the British Museum, 4 vols., 1898–1907, III, p. 39.

Thomas Lawrence was 22 in 1791, and was as eager as any other portrait artist to see Emma. He wrote to Samuel Lysons, the well-known antiquarian, 'A particular friend of mine promised to get me introduced at Sir William Hamilton's to see this wonderful woman you have doubtless heard of – Mrs Hart. He has succeeded; but has unfortunately made an appointment for that purpose on Sunday next, at half-past ten. What shall I do? I hear it is the most gratifying thing to a painter's eye that can be; and I am frightened at the same time with the intimation that she will soon be Lady Hamilton, and that I may not have such another opportunity. . . .' From such a punctilious observor of etiquette, as Thomas Lawrence, such a plea to be released from a previous appointment was going far indeed.

A print after the drawing exists. Made in 1792 by C. Knight for Lawrence an impression in the British Museum is inscribed in pencil beneath the word 'Emma'. 'Wrote by the Lady/This was drawn in pencil by Sir T. Lawrence while in company with Lady Hamilton and engraved for his private use by C. Knight.' (Inscribed impression *Repr.* facing p. 29, George Somes Layard, *Sir Thomas Lawrence's Letter-Bag*, London, George Allen, 1906.)

58   Five Pieces from the Clarence dinner service
porcelain, Barr, Flight & Barr, Royal Porcelain Works, Worcester, 1790–2
painted by James Pennington with figures of Hope once said to represent Lady Hamilton
four oval dishes, 11 x 8in (28 x 20·3cm)
one soup plate, diameter
10 in (25·4cm)
lent by the National Maritime Museum, Greenwich

PROV: William IV; ? Lord A. Fitzclarence; the Earl of Errol (sold from his collection as having been *a.* presented to Nelson by the Nation; *b.* representations of Lady Hamilton as 'Hope'); the late Revd Hugh Nelson-Ward.

EXH: Loan collection of Nelson relics in aid of the *Save the Victory* fund, Spink & Son Ltd., 1928, No. 31.

The dinner service was made for the Duke of Clarence by Flight of Worcester 1790–2. Each piece bears 'The sea, with a Ship of War in the distance and a figure of Hope in the foreground'. All are bordered by a blue and gold radiating pattern. It is extremely unlikely that the painted figures represent

Emma Hamilton, although her classical Attitudes may have suggested the variety of poses adopted. The Duke of Clarence, Prince William Henry (later William IV) had been a naval colleague and friend of Nelson's in the West Indies. He had stood witness to Nelson's first marriage. His own libidinous life was such that legends of the most romantic sort, including this one of Emma's being represented on the dinner service, only too easily grew up. Emma had captured the popular imagination.

Jean Baptiste Monnoyer (1636–99)
and Sir Thomas Lawrence
(1769–1830)
59   Lady Hamilton as a Bacchante
oil on canvas, 67 x 50in (170·2 x 127cm)
lent from the Broadlands Collection

PROV: Sir Joshua Reynolds; by him given to the Second Viscount Palmerston; by descent to the present owners.

LIT: Baily, *Repr.*, facing p. 116 (as after Lawrence); Connell, pp. 250–6, *Repr.*, facing p. 256.

The portrait of Emma was the third and final painting to be executed within the seventeenth-century garland of flowers. Having been on friendly terms with the second Viscount Palmerston for over a quarter of a century, Sir Joshua Reynolds, towards the end of his life, presented him with an enigmatical painting to hang in the alcove above his sideboard in the dining-room at Broadlands. It was a canvas subsequently identified by Palmerston as having been painted by Jean Baptiste Monnoyer. When acquired by Sir Joshua it showed a Roman Charity surrounded by the wreath of flowers. Reynolds painted over the Charity, substituting a rebus intended as a puzzle for and compliment to Palmerston: an eye painted in the middle of a hand, signifying Liberality guided by Sagacity. Palmerston evidently did not like the picture, and found it an embarrassment. In a letter to his wife, written on 1 December 1790, he said 'I sat an hour with Sir Joshua and Miss Palmer yesterday morning, who are both well. I told him pretty nearly my opinion upon the subject of the picture, resting as much as I could upon the unpleasant feel I should have in putting up a picture which must excite so much curiosity, and which must be explained into a compliment to myself. He was very good humoured about it and said the hand might easily be rubbed out, and the space left vacant, or anything else put in. I am to dine with him on Saturday . . .' (Quoted by Connell, p. 253.) The picture had been sent to London for cleaning when Reynolds became so ill that he could no longer contemplate painting. He died on the 23 February 1792, but the painting had already been put in the hands of the young Thomas Lawrence to whom Palmerston eventually paid 30gns for adding the figure of a Bacchante, half-length. Palmerston had been full of enthusiasm when he met the Hamiltons in Paris in the autumn of 1791. Certainly Emma seems to have typified for the British the archetypal Bacchante. The painting which has hung in its destined alcove at Broadlands ever since, has traditionally been identified as a portrait of Lady Hamilton. (Information supplied from Broadlands by Mr John Barratt.)

Married life

Emma was never received at the English Court and therefore could not represent the English Queen as an official Embassy hostess. But, married, she was perfectly acceptable to the majority of English travellers. There were hoards of them in Naples in the 1790s, for the troubles in France had closed many other tourist areas, and Naples remained for almost the entire decade the most peaceful centre for Grand Tourists.

In the autumn of 1791 the second Viscount Palmerston met the new Lady Hamilton in Paris and wrote to his wife: 'She is very handsome but not elegant, her face is very much like what I have seen in a fine old portrait and she wears her hair something in that style. She seems very good humoured, very happy and very attentive to him.' (Connell, 248.) In 1793 Lady Palmerston herself accompanied her husband to Naples and on 16 January reported to her brother Benjamin Mee: 'I there was presented to Lady Hamilton, *pour la première fois.* I find her not so beautiful as I expected, but certainly extremely handsome and her figure uncommonly fine. She was well dressed and there is something in her manner very good humoured and a great desire of pleasing. . . . She is extremely obliging, without the least appearance of feeling any elevation from the change in her situation. Sir William perfectly idolises her and I do not wonder he is proud of so magnificent a marble, belonging so entirely to himself.' (Connell, 276.) Sir William too was able to write on 17 April 1792 to Horace Walpole of 'Lady H. who has had also a difficult part to act & has succeeded wonderfully, having gained by having no pretentions, the thorough approbation of all the English ladies. The Queen of Naples, as you may have heard, was very kind to her on our return, and treats her like any other travelling lady of distinction; in short, we are very comfortably situated here.' (Morrison, I, 166.)

60

Ferdinando IV and Maria
Carol na
blue ceramic roundels with white
profile portraits in relief, framed
together in ormolu
frame, height 5 5/16 in (13·5cm)
width 9 3/8 in (23·8cm)
*lent by the Museo Correale di Terranova,
Sorrento*

The Neapolitan Court, particularly under the influence of Maria Carolina, favoured Great Britain as an ally. Britain's maritime supremacy now offered protection against attack from France: Maria Carolina dreaded nothing more than the fate of her sister Marie Antoinette. English things became the rage. These ceramic portrait medallions in blue and white were probably made in imitation of Wedgwood and English taste.

61

*Konrad Heinrich Schweikle
(1779–1833)*
Maria Carolina
white marble
height 22½in (57·2cm)
width 11 5/8 in (29·5cm)
depth 8 5/8 in (22cm)
signed (on base at right): *Schweickle
machte mich*
lent by the Heim Gallery (London) Ltd

Those who did not sympathise with Maria Carolina saw in her the dominant and aggressive personality ruling the Kingdom of the two Sicilies. Her pro-British policies were seconded by her chief Minister, the ex-patriot Briton, Sir John Acton. (Cat. No. 63.) Maria Carolina the politician saw in the new Lady Hamilton a tool through which to manipulate Sir William and thus have an opportunity to influence British policy in her own favour.

62

Costanzo Angelini (1760–1853)
Queen Maria Carolina
pastel, 19 11/16 x 15 3/4 in (50 x 40cm)
signed (lower r): *C. Angelini*
lent by the Museo di San Martino, Naples

PROV: Giovanni Tesorone; acquired by the Museo Nazionale di San Martino, 25 May 1909.
Maria Carolina, of whom Emma was to grow so fond, never had an ideal face or figure. (See notes to Cat. No. 36.) She was almost 40 when Emma returned to Naples as Lady Hamilton, and she must have looked rather as she does in this pastel.

63

Giovanni M. Griffoni
Sir John Acton
oil on canvas, 29 x 24in (73·6 x 61cm)

63 cont.

inscribed: *Sir John Acton Bart. Born 1736 died 1st August 1811. Buried at Palermo.*

lent by Sir Robert Throckmorton, Bt

PROV: From the collection of Lady Acton, wife of Sir John; by descent to their daughter Elizabeth, Lady Throckmorton; and thence by descent to the present owner.

EXH: Royal Academy, Winter Exhibition, 1960, No. 214.

General Sir John Francis Edward Acton was one of those eighteenth-century anomalies, a Catholic of English extraction born of a French mother in Besancon in 1736 during the political uncertainties of Jacobite hopes. He was christened with names honouring the Stuart pretenders whose cause was to be dead before he reached manhood. Stigmatised by his middle names, if by nothing else, he sought a career working for the Catholic powers of Europe, first France, then Tuscany and finally the Kingdom of the Two Sicilies.

His allegiance was entirely abroad yet, ironically, he succeeded to the ancient baronetcy of his distant Shropshire family and took pleasure in being known as General Sir John Acton. Soon after his arrival in Naples Sir William approved of him and enthusiastically reported to the Secretary of State in London 'I flatter myself I have had the good fortune to gain his confidence and esteem. He is certainly a very sensible man and has the character of an excellent Sea Officer.' (BM Egerton MSS. 2636, fo. 261.) From 1780 until his final recall to England in 1800 Hamilton could thus enjoy the confidence of the man who soon rose to be chief Minister of the Kingdom.

At certain moments in his career Acton seemed the supreme power in Naples. He was credited at one time with being the Queen's lover. Certainly the Queen approved of the fact that he was a bachelor, and if amorous adventures did increase his powers, he was fortunate in never falling from favour. On the eve of Sir William's departure in 1800 Sir John out-did him in making a marriage to startle society. He was granted dispensation to allow him to marry his niece: he was then 64 years old, and she slightly less than 14. He had never been married before.

64

Philip Hackert (1734–1807)
The English Garden, Caserta
1792
tempera, $18\frac{7}{8}$ x $39\frac{3}{4}$in (48 x 101cm)
signed: *nel Giardino inglese a Caserta Filippo Hackert depinta* 1792
in original gilded bronze box frame: one of a series of seven tempera paintings by Hackert showing views of the Royal Palaces
lent by the Palazzo Reale, Caserta

PROV: Collezione Borbonica.

EXH: *Il passaggio Nepolitana nella Pittura . . .*, Naples, 1962, No. 45, *Repr.* IX; Vienna, 1969.

LIT: F. De Filippis and O. Morisani, *Pittori tedeschi a Napoli nel Settecento*, Naples,

1943; H. Geller, 150 *Jahre deutsche Landschafts Malerei*, Dresden, 1951.

To make an English garden in the grounds of the Royal Palace at Caserta had been the idea of Sir William Hamilton, and for many years it remained one of his greatest interests. The Neapolitan royal family had long held him as a valued friend as well as Minister and when he returned to Naples in the autumn of 1784 after an almost eighteen-month absence in England he found them very willing to adopt his attractive suggestion. To his friend Sir Joseph Banks he wrote on 20 February 1785: 'The Queen of Naples has adopted my project and has given me the commission to send for a British Gardener and Nursery-man. . . . the Queen does me the honour to give me the Superintendence of her Garden.' (Fothergill, p. 205, quoting BM Add. MSS. 34048, fo. 22.) To this request Banks responded by sending out an able gardener called Graffer, who found the task so attractive that he settled happily despite his initial ignorance of Italian and his wife and family's unhappy status as exiles.

The garden nestles in a well-watered piece of rolling ground to the right of the extreme end of the three kilometre panoramic drive from the immense Palace towards the hills at Caserta. It seems a romantic oasis even today. In its prime it must have been one of the most successful small-scale landscaping achievements of the English eighteenth century – if a piece of ground 'upwards of fifty acres' may be termed small. That it was a recreational source of delight, and not merely a botanical achievement in that rather torrid climate, is certain. On 2 June 1793, the year after Hackert depicted it, Emma reported to Charles Greville from Caserta: 'For political reasons we have lived eight months at Caserta . . . the English garden is going on very fast, the King and Queen go there every day. Sir Wm. & me are there every morning at seven a clock, some-times dine there & allways drink tea, in short, it is Sir Wms. favourite child & boath him & me are now studying botany but not to make ourselves pedantical prigs to shew our learning like some of our traveling neighbours, but for our own pleasure. Greffer is as happy as a prince . . .' (Morrison, I, p. 177.) The recreational aspect of the garden is indicated in Hackert's painting: a group of three women, a child and a dog are shown in the left foreground. Sir William too had a view of the English Garden by Hackert hanging in the Palazzo Sessa.

<table>
<tr><td valign="top">65</td><td>

Fruit cooler decorated with view
of Palazzo della Regina
Giovanna, Posillipo
porcelain, Real Fabbrica, Naples
height 15¾in (40cm)
width 9 1/16 in (23cm)
inscribed: *Veduta del Palazzo della Rega.
Giovanna a Posillipo*

lent by the Museo di Capodimonte, Naples

</td></tr>
</table>

PROV: Collezione Borbonica.

Grand porcelain such as this from the Royal Collection could only have become familiar to Emma after her return to Naples in the autumn of 1791. This fruit cooler shows a view she must have known at Posillipo, which she and Sir

William often visited to stay at their sea-side house, the Villa Emma. (See Cat. No. 38.)

66

Tureen decorated with a view of Posillipo
porcelain, Real Fabbrica, Naples
height 7½in (19cm)
width 9 1/16 in (23cm)
inscribed: *Veduta della punta di Posillipo*

lent by the Museo di Capodimonte, Naples

See notes on Cat. No. 65.

67

Tureen decorated with a view of the Palazzo di Portici
porcelain, Real Fabbrica, Naples
height 15¾in (40cm)
width 13in (33cm)
inscribed: *Veduta del Palazzo di Portici di S.M.*

lent by the Museo di Capodimonte, Naples

PROV: Collezione Borbonica.

A fine piece of Royal porcelain showing Portici, the Royal Palace south of Naples, close to Vesuvius and the ancient buried towns of Herculaneum and Pompeii. Here the King had established a Royal museum to show the antique works of art discovered in the course of excavations. Sir William Hamilton also had a house at Portici, the Villa Angelica, close to the Royal Palace. He himself acquired, often illicitly one suspects, antique works of art from the excavations. Goethe records a fascinating incident. On one occasion when he was taken by Hackert to Sir William's 'Sir William showed us his secret treasure vault, which was crammed with works of art and junk, all in the greatest confusion. Oddments from every period, busts, torsos, vases, bronzes, decorative implements of all kinds made of Sicilian agate, carvings, paintings and chance bargains of every sort, lay about all higgledy-piggledy; there was even a small chapel. Out of curiosity I lifted the lid of a long case which lay on the floor and in it were two magnificent candelabra. I nudged Hackert and asked him in a whisper if they were not very like the candelabra in the Portici museum. He silenced me with a look.' (Goethe, pp. 310–11.)

68

Tureen decorated with a view of Portici
porcelain, Real Fabbrica, Naples
height 7½in (19cm)
width 9 1/16 in (23cm)
lent by the Museo di Capodimonte, Naples

PROV: Collezione Borbonica.
See notes on Cat. No. 67.

69

Travelling case of porcelain
decorated in the antique style
porcelain, Real Fabbrica, Naples
gold, white, black and terracotta painted
decoration
lent by the Museo di Capodimonte, Naples

PROV: Collezione Borbonica.
A Royal travelling case of fine porcelain sufficient to serve one person with chocolate. It is decorated in the antique taste popularised by Sir William's own publications: *D'Hancarville* (P. F. Hugues), *Collection of Etruscan, Greek and Roman Antiquities from the Cabinet of the Hon Wm. Hamilton*, four vols., Naples, 1766–7; the second collection was written up by Sir William Hamilton himself *Collection of Engravings from Ancient Vases mostly of Pure Greek Workmanship discovered in Sepulchres in the Kingdom of the Two Sicilies*, four vols., Naples, 1791–5. Sir William's two collections brought about a revolution in taste and appear to have offered Neo-classical vase painters a pattern book. Josiah Wedgwood was among those who benefited. He wrote to Sir William in 1787: 'The whole nation, as well as I, have long spoken with gratitude of the patronage you have afforded, and the assistance you have given, to the artists in this country by the introduction of so many of the valuable relics of antiquity.' (A. Finer and G. Savage, *Selected Letters of Josiah Wedgwood*, London, 1965, p. 307.) Such tributes must have helped to give Emma a proprietary feeling about the development of the Neo-classical style. She too could use the engraved plates as a pattern book when devising her Attitudes.

70

Moeurs coutumes des Romains
par M. Bridault, Maitre de Pension,
Paris, P. G. Le Mercier, 1754
8vo., sheep
inscribed (on half-title): *Given to Lady
Hamilton by her dear friend the Queen of
Naples at Caserta 1794*

*lent by the National Maritime Museum,
Greenwich*

PROV: the late Revd Hugh Nelson-Ward.
EXH: Loan collection of Nelson relics in aid of the *Save the Victory* fund, Spink & Son Ltd., 1928, No. 60.
That Emma was both on friendly terms with the Queen of Naples, and bent on studying ancient costume and manners is indicated by this book, proudly inscribed by Emma.

71

Angelica Kauffmann (1741–1807)
Lady Hamilton
oil on canvas, 18 x 13⅜in (45·8 x 34cm)
inscribed (on the back of the stretcher):
Emma, Lady Hamilton, Naples, 1796

lent by the Victoria and Albert Museum

PROV: Bought from a dealer in 1875; no recorded provenance.
EXH: *Famous British Women Artists*, Sheffield Art Gallery, September–October 1953; *Angelika Kauffmann und ihre Zeitgenossen*, Bregenz, July–October 1968, and Vienna, November–February 1968–9, No. 274, *Repr.*, pl. 53. (As copy of Angelica Kauffmann.)

Angelica Kauffmann's portrait of Emma as the Comic Muse was to become the sitter's favourite representation of herself. Unlike Vigée-Le Brun, Angelica Kauffmann seems to have possessed an extremely winning personality. Sir William, Goethe and Emma alike all looked forward to seeing her again. Immediately on Emma's arrival in Naples Sir William promised that Angelica should paint her at the first opportunity. (See Emma's letter to Greville, 22 July 1786, Morrison, I, p. 117.) There is however about Angelica's portraits a Neo-classical sameness: Fuseli, her friend and genuine admirer, was caustic upon this point: 'The male and female characters of Angelica never vary in form, features and expression, from the favourite ideal she had composed in her mind . . . Her heroines are herself; and whilst suavity of countenance and aluring graces shall be able to divert the general eye from the sterner demands of character and expression, can never fail to please.' (Pilkington, p. 638.) Perhaps this was why Emma was so pleased: she saw herself as the acme of fashion, a perfect representation of the best contemporary taste.

If this portrait was indeed painted in 1796 as the inscription on the back of the stretcher claims, there is no mystery as to why it is not recorded in the Hamilton correspondence. By that time the devastations of the French were already feared. On 7 June Sir William wrote to Greville, 'I must own to you that I think that Italy is in great danger of being completely plunder'd and ruin'd unless some unforseen accident should operate in its favour, and that very soon . . . What a pity that Italy shou'd be robbed of its finest marbles, pictures & bronzes, which you see by what has happen'd at Parma will certainly be the case shou'd the French marauders advance.' (Morrison, I, pp. 220 and 221.) Emma when she wrote to Greville was no longer a girl who chattered about which painter was currently working on her portrait. She was by now 31, an intimate friend of the Queen of Naples and a valuable aid to Sir William upon whom the worsening political situation thrust an unaccustomed burden. On 21 September 1796 Emma wrote 'We have not time to write to you as we have been three days and nights writing to send by this courrier letters of *consequence* for our government. They ought to be grateful to Sir William and *myself in particular*, as my situation at this Court is very extra-ordinary, and what no person as as yet arrived at; but one as no thanks, and I am allmost sick of grandeur.

'We are tired to death with anxiety, and God knows where we shall soon be, and what will become of us, if things go on as they do now.' (Morrison, I, p. 225.)

Nelson and Neapolitan politics

It was into this atmosphere of intrigue, power politics and Emma's own new found sense of filling a key position in Naples that Nelson sailed.

He had first visited the Hamiltons on 11 September 1793 as a direct result of a treaty of alliance negotiated by Hamilton and Acton between their two countries. He came seeking Neapolitan troops to support Admiral Hood in the occupation of Toulon. On that occasion he had spent four days in Naples, and had been entertained most flatteringly both by the Hamiltons and by Ferdinando IV. Sir William obviously took to him at once, and urged Emma to entertain him as cordially as possible. It was Sir William who kept up a correspondence both friendly and official with Nelson for the next five years, until in fact he returned in urgent need of permission to water and revictual his ships at Neapolitan ports. The Kingdom of the Two Sicilies had recently signed a treaty of neutrality with France. They had undertaken not to permit access to more than one British warship at a time to any port. With Emma's aid this embargo was overcome. The vexed question of whether she effected what otherwise would have been impossible is not one which we have to answer here. The important point is that Emma, Sir William and Nelson himself all believed that without her intercession with the Queen the British fleet might never have been allowed to take on the supplies without which Nelson might have been unable to catch up with the vast French fleet and destroy it so successfully in Aboukir Bay.

So far as one can tell, Nelson had not seen the Hamiltons since those four days in 1793. Yet, at the moment of his great triumph he wrote to them in gratitude. To Emma he wrote: 'You and Sir William have spoiled me . . . I trust my mutilations will not cause me to be less welcome. They are the marks of honour.' (Pettigrew, I, p. 140.) This, if nothing else, is proof that they had not met for five years. In 1793 Nelson was a hale and able-bodied man; in 1798 he was not. At the siege of Calvi in Corsica in 1794 he had lost the sight of his right eye. On 24 July 1797, storming Santa Cruz in Tenerife, he had lost his right arm. These, surely, rather than the forehead wound he sustained in Egypt were the mutilations he referred to. Emma was so ecstatic about having helped in an heroic enterprise that she fainted when she read his letter with the news which arrived on 3 September. Nothing could have seemed more thrilling to her than to welcome the Hero of the Nile. Immediately she began to work with all the showmanship in her nature on a fittingly festal welcome for the conqueror. Nelson himself, after years of routine at sea, loved a good show, particularly when allied to real warmth and praise. He returned from Egypt and walked straight into the arms of Sir William and Emma. Emma entered history.

Naples was the first friendly port that Nelson's fleet entered after the Battle of the Nile. Although some British ships were badly crippled, fifteen out of the nineteen French men-of-war had either been destroyed or captured. The British were virtual masters of the Mediterranean; and the Kingdom of the Two Sicilies became safe from attack by sea. The Royal Family were as delighted as anyone, despite the uneasy treaty of neutrality their country had made with the French Republic. Ever since her sister, Marie Antoinette, had been guillotined on 16 October 1793, Maria Carolina had personally borne an implacable hatred for the French nation. Sir William and Emma had prepared a room in their house for Nelson. He was exhausted and weak, having lost much blood when a shot cut away the skin on his forehead: for a time he had thought that his end had come. Emma nursed him, worshipped him, and foresaw an assured future for him as the saviour of Europe. His wife had nursed him devotedly a year earlier, after the amputation of his right arm; but one suspects that she had constantly urged him to use the mutilation as an excuse for giving up his career. Far from irking him in this way, Emma nursed him as the hope of his country and all Europe, spurring him on to further greatness. This chimed with Nelson's own ambitions. Emma may also have been the first woman with whom he had come into close contact since the loss of his arm who had not treated him as a mutilated wreck. She was also still extremely attractive. Early in October he wrote to Admiral Lord St Vincent, and ended the letter 'I am writing opposite Lady Hamilton, therefore you will not be surprised at the glorious jumble of this letter. Were your Lordship in my place, I much doubt if you could write so well; our hearts and our hands must be all a flutter: Naples is a dangerous place, and we must keep clear of it.' (*Nelson's Letters*, ed. by Geoffrey Rawson, 1960, p. 207.) His officers and superiors began to worry about the undue and (they feared) unprincipled influence being brought to bear on Nelson in favour of the Kingdom of the Two Sicilies.

Naturally, but foolishly, he began to think of himself as practically in-vincible, even in fields not his own. He won over Sir William to urge Ferdinando and his troops, under the Austrian General Mack, to march upon the French in Rome. The expedition was a fiasco, and the British Government found it hard to forgive Sir William or Nelson for their parts in it. However it was not the moment to rebuke a hero publicly. An unofficial whipping-boy had to be found to relieve British feelings: the official mind chose Emma for this rôle. In fairness to her, one has to point out that she was not the pernicious influence which the popular mind was led to suppose, urging Nelson on to unparalleled acts of fool-hardy indiscretion. Nelson was by nature reckless. His self-reliance and over-confidence had given trouble before. As a midshipman on an Arctic expedition, he had left his ship without permission, to chase a polar bear with the butt end of his musket; in the West Indies in 1784 he had put in jeopardy the planters' willing allegiance to the British Crown by attempting to interrupt their trade with the seceding American States. Long before his involvement in Naples he had become well known for taking the law into his own hands: when he was victorious it was glory won by unorthodox tactics, but his failures could seem like dismal examples of mismanagement. He had been expressly ordered not to go ashore at Tenerife, but he did so; and he lost his arm.

Britain may also have had another worry: the ascendency of Napoleon was, to the old order, a terrifying example of a man from the ranks rising to the top by sheer force of personality and military ability, until he took over supreme

command of the entire nation. A good officer led his men by personal magnetism and direct command, and if he did not himself obey orders from his
superiors he was a potential menace just as strong as the force at his command.
This may have been why Nelson was not given official rewards as great as those
of his colleagues. Admiral Sir John Jervis was created Earl of St Vincent for
commanding the action of that name in which the Spanish fleet was defeated
in 1797: for his success at the Battle of the Nile Nelson was only made a Baron.
Fears of Nelson's so forgetting his allegiance as to start issuing orders or even
making political decisions without official sanction, must always have been at
the back of the British Government's mind.

In Naples Nelson gave a fine display of disregard for orders. The whole
conduct of the campaign to recapture Naples after it had fallen to the Jacobins
was extraordinary by British standards. When Nelson sailed to blockade the
town he had on board not only Sir William, but Emma. And when on 13 July,
in the midst of assisting to restore Ferdinando IV to his throne, Nelson received
orders from Lord Keith, his superior in the Mediterranean, to take his fleet to
the defence of Minorca, he defied the orders. From that moment on he was in
particularly bad odour with the Board of Admiralty. (See Naish, pp. 473–4.)
Emma was blamed more and more.

72

Anonymous
Nelson wounded at the Nile
1798
oil on canvas, 33 x 25½in (83·9 x 64·8cm)
lent by the National Maritime Museum,
Greenwich (Greenwich Hospital Collection)

PROV: Sent by Nelson to Lady Parker, wife of Admiral Sir Peter Parker; bequeathed by her daughter to the Painted Hall Collection, Greenwich Hospital; transferred to the National Maritime Museum in 1934 as part of the Greenwich Hospital Collection.

LIT: Lord Charles Beresford and H. W. Wilson, *Nelson and his Times*, *Repr.*, p. 101; Hardwick, *Repr.*, facing p. 73.

Nelson sent this portrait showing him as he must have appeared, wounded, after the Battle of the Nile, to the wife of Admiral Sir Peter Parker, an old and helpful friend of both the Nelsons. His forehead bound up, his right eye blinded, his arm gone, this is very much as he must have appeared to the Hamiltons when he sailed into the Bay of Naples on 22 September 1798. Though victorious, they had limped back from Egypt, *Vanguard*, Nelson's flagship, arriving in tow. Cornelia Knight, an English lady staying in Naples at the time, reported: 'Admiral Nelson is little, and not remarkable in his person either way; but he has great animation of countenance, and activity in his appearance: his manners are unaffectedly simple and modest.' (Cornelia Knight, *Autobiography*, I, p. 115.) Nelson was a hero of almost 40, Sir William an Envoy of almost 70, and Emma a warm-hearted enthusiast of 33.

73

Silver gilt cup presented to
Lord Nelson by Lady Hamilton
1798
height 3½in (8·9cm)
diameter 3⅛in (8·2cm)
lent by the Victory Museum, Portsmouth

Emma herself must have presented Nelson with this cup as a keepsake in the autumn he spent with them after the Battle of the Nile. One of the bequests in Nelson's will reads 'To Emma, Lady Hamilton the silver cup marked E.H. which she presented to him.'

After Nelson's death the cup was returned to Emma, and she had engraved on its side this inscription 'THIS CUP was PRESENTED/ By Emma, Lady Hamilton to/ Dear Admiral Lord Nelson,/ The Victorious Hero of the Nile;/ 29th Septr. 1798./ Who constantly drank out of it/ Until the Glorious tho' fatal/ 21st Octr. 1805./ And bequeathed by his Lordships/ Will to the Donor.'

74

John Thomas Serres (1759–1825)
Nelson and Emma at Posillipo
oil on canvas,
23¼ x 35½in (59·1 x 90·2cm)
signed (on awning of boat): . . *ERRES*
lent by the National Trust (Fairhaven
Collection, Anglesey Abbey)

At Posillipo there were shipbuilding yards as well as seductive holiday areas. What could be more natural than that Nelson should visit the Villa Emma, and also inspect the building of boats? It was his duty to refit the British fleet, making good losses sustained during the Battle of the Nile. The Neapolitans idolised him and many representations were made of him in 1798. Emma had soon become familiar as his constant companion. Colletta, the nineteenth-century historian of Naples, gives an account of the reviewing of troops before the ill-fated expedition against Rome. 'The King had taken up his quarters in this camp, prepared to march with the army; the Queen, attired in a riding-habit, constantly drove along the lines in a chariot and four, accompanied by the ambassadors from friendly sovereigns, and other foreigners of distinction, the barons of the Kingdom, and Lady Hamilton, who under pretence of escorting Her Majesty, displayed her own beauty in all its magnificence to the camp, and paraded her conquest over the victor of Aboukir who, seated beside her in the same carriage, appeared fascinated and submissive to her charms.' (General Pietro Colletta, *History of the Kingdom of Naples 1734–1825*, trans. S. Horner, Edinburgh, 1858, pp. 250–1.) That Emma should have been depicted in company with Nelson was natural, and must have given pleasure to them both. Discretion was not an early ingredient of their relationship. Serres, maritime painter to George III, the Duke of Clarence, and the Admiralty, was posted around the Mediterranean to depict naval installations of importance to Great Britain.

75
Plate VI, A & B

Memorial and Mourning pendant
enamel, seed pearls, coloured glass, silver, hair, etc.
$2\frac{7}{8}$ x $2\frac{7}{16}$ in (7·2 x 6·2cm)
recto: trophy (damaged) symbolising Nelson's destruction of the French fleet in Aboukir Bay, enclosed in a lock of Nelson's hair. With a cartouche in seed pearls and enamel
inscribed: *1st Augt. 98*
verso: locks of hair enclosing oval medallion in enamel and seed pearls
inscribed: *Prince Albert died in my Arms 25th Decr. 1798*
lent by the Victory Museum, Portsmouth

After the disastrous expedition against Rome, the Neapolitan army was driven back upon the Kingdom of the Two Sicilies. The Royal Family, in terror at the advance of the French, decided they must flee to Sicily. The Hamiltons organised the escape, by means of Nelson's fleet. To allay suspicion of flight the Hamiltons made almost no preparations and abandoned all their possessions – with the exception of Sir William's collection which had already been crated up earlier in the year. The Neapolitan mob was in a state of hysteria. Had they got wind of the Royal plan to abandon them they would have resisted it with violence. In preparing the escape Emma acted as go-between, carrying messages from the Queen to Sir William and Nelson. The embarkation was successful and *Vanguard* sailed from Naples on 23 December 1798. A storm blew up worse than any Nelson had experienced in his life. Emma, one of the few who did not suffer from sea-sickness, nursed the Royal Family incessantly, particularly Maria Carolina's youngest son, the 6-year-old Prince Carlo Alberto who suffered from convulsions. On 25 December he had to be nursed all day, and although he seemed a little better at lunch-time, by evening he was exhausted and died in Emma's arms.

Emma must have had the pendant made in joint memory of the Battle of the Nile and the death of Prince Alberto, a lock of Nelson's hair on one side and of the Prince's on the other. The association seems singularly inappropriate and can only have been made because of her desire to commemorate her own intimate connection with heroes and royalty – an unwinning witness to in-sensitive vain-glory.

76

Anonymous
Maria Carolina in mourning
23⅝ x 18⅛in (60 x 46cm)
lent by the Museo di San Martino, Naples

Maria Carolina was stricken with grief at the death of her little son and could not bear to make a public appearance when they arrived in Palermo. Ferdinando alone landed with ceremonial pomp. This mourning picture of the Queen must have been made in 1799.

77

Decree of the Provisional
Government of Repubblica
Napoletana
official printed form filled out in manuscript
(signed by the War Minister, Gabriele
Manthone), *instructions for issuing rations
of wine to the troops, 15 May 1799*
8¼ x 13in (21 x 33cm)
*lent by the Museo di San Martino (Arch.
Storico), Naples*

After the flight of the Royal Family to Sicily the French captured Naples, savagely suppressing all resistance. On 23 January 1799 they set up the Parthenopean Republic. This was served by a provisional government of French officials and middle- and upper-class anti-royalists. It proved a bureau-cratic failure, running into a multitude of minor difficulties. Forms were printed, as here, on which to write the decrees of the provisional government. But enforcement of these decrees proved far from easy, as the Kingdom of the Two Sicilies had never enjoyed any measure of that logic and order which had characterised France since the days of Louis XIV. The resulting confusion made it easier for Ferdinando to win back Naples for a while.

78

Attributed to Costanzo Angelini
(1760–1853)
Cardinal Ruffo (1744–1827)

78 cont.

black and white chalks on grey paper,
$7\frac{7}{8}$ x $7\frac{1}{16}$ in (20 x 18cm)
lent by the Museo di San Martino, Naples

PROV: Principe Fabrizio Ruffo di Bagnara; given to the Museo di San Martino 25 June 1910.

Fabrizio Ruffo was a Calabrian of noble family. He had worked as an administrator in the Papal See and had had experience both as treasurer and war minister under Pope Pius VI. The French having driven the Pope into exile, Ruffo had returned home and was at hand to rally support for King Ferdinando IV who created him Vicar General on 25 January. With a small band of companions Ruffo set up the Royal Standard on the mainland on 7 February. Appealing both to patriotism and religious convictions, he soon raised a popular army, a wild, undisciplined and ferocious band 17,000 strong. They marched almost unopposed on Naples. Simultaneously the Austrians declared war on France. Prudently the French army began to withdraw from Naples.

Anonymous

79

Cardinal Ruffo handing the flag to the people
pen and grey wash on paper,
$16\frac{15}{16}$ x $22\frac{13}{16}$ in (43 x 58cm)
inscribed (lower r but so damaged by water that it is impossible to read in full)
lent by the Museo di San Martino, Naples

PROV: Enrico Ferrara Dentice, Naples; given to the Museo di San Martino 12 August 1934.

EXH: *Mostra storica dell' Unita d'Italia,* Turin, 1961, No. 88.

Cardinal Ruffo had raised an army which conquered without reference to military or political conventions. The agreements which he made with it, and indeed the peace treaty which he made with the rebels when he arrived in Naples, were equally unorthodox. Nelson and Ferdinando accepted Ruffo's success, but not the terms on which he had achieved it. They overruled his lenient treaty and punished the rebels mercilessly. Nelson has always been criticised for sanctioning this injustice; and blame for much of the brutality has been laid on Emma's passionate nature. But such was Maria Carolina's passionate hatred of the French, and Ferdinando's desire to reassert his temporarily despised authority that, considering the quick tempered revengeful nature of the people they ruled over, it becomes impossible to judge the situation by phlegmatic British standards. Without Nelson and the Hamiltons things might even have been worse.

80

The arrival of Ferdinando IV aboard *Fordroyant*
medal, bronze – both plain and gilded examples of this medal exist
diameter $1\frac{15}{16}$ in (4·9cm)
lent by the Museo di San Martino, Naples

PROV: Eduardo Ricciardi, Naples; given to the Museo di San Martino, 21 November 1921.

LIT: Eduardo Ricciardi, *Medaglie del Regno delle Due Sicilie 1735–1861*, Napoli, 1930, p. 23.

On 10 July 1799 Ferdinando IV took up quarters aboard *Foudroyant*, Nelson's ship, and in this he returned to Naples. He remained on her for almost a month, never going ashore. Accompanied by Sir William and Emma he held Court on board, saw his Royal Standards flying from the battlements of the Neapolitan forts, and satisfied himself that his chastened and once more submissive subjects were at least theoretically loyal. On 5 August they left the Bay of Naples to land in triumph at Palermo on the 8th.

81

Embroidered hem with the motifs 'Nelson – Bronte – Nelson'
muslin embroidered with silk, gold threads and sequins by Sicilian embroideresses
10 x 34in (25·4 x 86·4cm)
lent by the National Maritime Museum, Greenwich

PROV: the late Revd Hugh Nelson-Ward.
LIT: Hardwick, p. 136.
Nelson was given the Dukedom of Brontë for his part in restoring Ferdinando IV to Naples in 1799. Emma must have had this embroidery done for a dress made in honour of Nelson. She may have worn it for the feast of the Patron Saint of Palermo, St Rosalia on 16 August. Maria Carolina then gave a fête in honour of Nelson and both the Hamiltons. Officially the gift of the Dukedom was made on 13 August, but no doubt Emma knew of it beforehand and had the dress embroidered between the time of her return to Palermo on 8 August and the festival eight days later.

82

Raffaello Gasparino
Cup and saucer decorated in black and gold with silhouette portraits of Ferdinando IV and Maria Carolina
cup, height 2½in (6·2cm)
diameter 2⅝in (6·7cm)
saucer, diameter 5⅝in (14·2cm)
inscribed (on face of saucer): *Simbole de notre attachment*

lent by the Museo di San Martino, Naples

PROV: Lord Roseberg.
EXH: *Il Risorgimento in Terra di Lavoro*, Caserta, 1961, Cat. p. 110.
LIT: Giuseppe Morazzoni, *Le Porcellane Italiane*, Milan, 1935, p. 365, *Repr.* XCVI.
After the temporary seizure of Naples, great efforts were made to reawaken

loyalty to the Bourbons. Maria Carolina and Ferdinando had to present a united front, despite the fact that the King was already deeply involved with Lucia Migliaccio, Duchessa di Floridia whom he eventually married after the Queen's death. (See Cat. No. 83.)

83 *Plate* VII, A	*Selvaggi* Lucia Migliaccio, Duchessa di Floridia oil on canvas, 3 $\frac{15}{16}$ in (10cm) signed (lower r): *Selvaggio* *lent by the Museo di San Martino, Naples*

PROV: Acquired by Ministero della Pubblica Instruzione, 1933, for the Museo di San Martino.

How far the taste promoted by Sir William and exemplified by Emma herself was adopted in Naples is demonstrated by this miniature of the lady who, after the death of Maria Carolina was to become the morganatic wife of Ferdinando IV. (Cf. Cat. No. 23.)

84	Enamel brooch with portrait in style of Emma Hamilton silver enamel and brilliants, 1 $\frac{3}{8}$ in (3·5cm) *lent by the Museo di Capodimonte, Naples* *(De Ciccio Collection)*

This brooch from the De Ciccio Collection, Naples, shows a lady, possibly Emma herself, dressed in another style popularised by her in Naples at the end of the eighteenth century.

85 *Plate* IV	*Leonardo Guzzardi* Nelson oil on canvas, 33 $\frac{7}{8}$ x 20 $\frac{1}{2}$ in (86 x 52cm) signed (lower l on shield): *Leonardus Guzzardi Pin.* 1799 *lent by the Museo di San Martino, Naples*

PROV: From the collection of the Palazzo Reale, Caserta; deposited in the Museo Nazionale di San Martino, Naples, 1948.

EXH: *Il Risorgimento in terra di lavoro*, Caserta, 1961, p. 69.

LIT: Gino Doria, Frederico Bologna, Guido Pannai, *Settecento Napoletano*, Turin, 1962, *Repr.* XII.

In the rejoicings which succeeded the recapitulation of Naples in July 1799 Nelson became the hero of the nation. He was neither an imposing nor a handsome man. In October 1799 Lord Elgin thought he looked old and noticed that he had lost his upper teeth. Nelson was to write to Emma in January 1801, 'You are kind and good to an old friend, with one arm, a broken head and no teeth.' (Quoted by Naish, p. 565.) However he enjoyed wearing full-dress uniform and all the orders that had been showered upon him. Here he wears, as well as his British orders, the aigrette, the diamond-studded *chelengk* or plume of honour presented to him by the Sultan of Turkey, but which he had omitted to ask Royal permission to wear even in 1800. (See Naish, p. 559.) Lady Elgin reported from Gibraltar 'they say there never was a man turned so *vain glorious* (that's the phrase) in the world as Lord N. He is now completely managed by Lady Hamilton.' (N. H. Grant, *The Letters of Mary . . . Countess of Elgin*, London, 1926, p. 17.)

There is a copy of this painting in the Maritime Museum, Greenwich.

86   Maltese Cross

$2\frac{13}{16} \times 1\frac{9}{16}$ in ($7\cdot1 \times 4$ cm)

lent by the Victory Museum, Portsmouth

Queen Maria Carolina, as fervid in her approval of Nelson and the English as she was frenzied with hatred of the French, appointed Emma as her deputy to receive the Maltese petitioners for aid. Emma was in the happy position of acting as Lady Bountiful to the Maltese, dispensing someone else's money. On 25 February 1800 she wrote to Greville: 'I have had a letter from the Emperor of Russia, with the Cross of Malta; Sir William has sent his Imperial Majesty's letter to Lord Grenville, to get me permission to wear it. I have rendered some service to the poor Maltese. I got them ten thousand pounds, and sent them corn when they were in distress. The deputies have been lodged at my house. I have been their Ambasadress, so his M. had rewarded me. If the King will give me leave to wear it abroad, it is of use to me. The Queen is having the order set in diamonds for me, but the one the Emperor sent is gold.' (Tours, p. 147.) Captain Ball, now Governor of Malta, was awarded the order at the same time. It is evident from the copy of a letter sent by Nelson to the Emperor of Russia, 26 February 1800 (Morrison, II, p. 88) that both the awards were made as a compliment to Nelson, who requested the distinction for his friends rather than himself. Emma received permission to wear the order and it appeared several times in subsequent portraits of her, notably that by J. Schmidt made at Dresden in 1800.

87   Two Gold Rings given to
           Lady Hamilton by Nelson,
           wedding ring and keeper

wedding ring diameter $\frac{5}{8}$ in ($1\cdot7$ cm)

keeper diameter $\frac{3}{4}$ in (2 cm)

lent by the Victory Museum, Portsmouth

Even before they set out for England in 1800, Nelson may have come to look upon Emma as his 'wife before God'. The fact that they were travelling with Sir William, and that Nelson was on his way back to England to his legal wife, seems to have made little difference either to his sense of propriety or to his self esteem. At what point he and Emma exchanged rings we do not know: it may have been after the death of Sir William. In the Maritime Museum, Greenwich, there is a similar clasped hand keeper worn by Nelson.

The relationship which the rings symbolised must have begun not later than the early months of 1800. On 23 April 1800 Emma and Sir William sailed with Nelson on *Foudroyant* to join the blockade of Malta. They treated it as a super pleasure cruise; and, judging from Nelson's letters of a year later, and Horatia's birth on 28 or 29 January 1801, for Nelson and Emma it was a honeymoon. On 23 April 1801 Nelson wrote to Emma: 'My dearest amiable friend, this day twelve months we sailed from Palermo on our tour to Malta. Ah! those were happy times: days of ease and nights of pleasure.' (Morrison, II, p. 142.)

88   **Ferdinando I** (after restoration
at end of Napoleonic wars)
brown and cream wax, profile portrait
in relief
diameter $4\frac{1}{2}$in ($11 \cdot 5$cm)
lent by the Museo di San Martino, Naples

PROV: Eduardo **Ric**cardi, Naples; given to the Museo di San Martino, 21 November 1921.

The Kingdom of the Two Sicilies had to suffer a much more serious period of French occupation before Ferdinando was once more permanently reinstated under the new title, Ferdinando I. Despite the efforts of Nelson and the Hamiltons the House of Bourbon would never be the same again. The Ferdinando who was eventually restored had almost become a man of the people. The days when Emma had basked in royal vain glory were over. The King was transformed into a man in a soft hat rather than a crown.

Sir William, Emma & Nelson

Nelson had hoped to sail home to England, and the Hamiltons had assumed that he would give them a passage on his ship. But England was at war, and Nelson not at the time on good terms with the Board of Admiralty. The Board did not permit him to withdraw one of the warships from the Mediterranean fleet in order to return home by sea. To his annoyance he was forced to travel overland. Sir William had been recalled by his government. After thirty-six years as British Envoy his final recall was disguised as 'home leave', but Hamilton must have suspected the truth although he valiantly continued to persuade himself that he would return shortly.

Maria Carolina decided to travel with them as far as Vienna. *Foudroyant* sailed for Leghorn on 10 June. The subsequent journey overland took four months; and Sir William suffered so much distress that his companions sometimes despaired of his reaching England alive. Everywhere they went people clamoured to see Nelson, the Hero of the Nile, and they gossiped about his obvious fascination with and for Emma Hamilton. The English were particularly sharp in their comments. Mrs St George remarked upon the laudatory songs in Nelson's honour composed by Miss Cornelia Knight and sung by Emma: 'She puffs the incense full in his face, but he receives it with pleasure, and snuffs it up very cordially.' (Mrs Richard Trench, *Remains*, London, 1862, pp. 105–12.) By the time that they reached Dresden Emma was over five months pregnant, so it is not surprising that there should have been cruel comments about her figure. Uncharitableness grew with her girth.

On 31 October, having waited in vain for a packet at Hamburg, they boarded a mail boat at Cuxhaven and sailed for England, reaching Great Yarmouth only on 6 November. For the moment they had escaped from circles of diplomatic incivility. Crowds of English countrymen welcomed Nelson ecstatically: unharnessing the horses from his carriage they pulled it triumphant through the streets. He had landed on home territory where people did not baulk at accepting Emma too.

But once arrived in London things were different. Still the crowds cheered, but gossip was unkind. Lady Nelson stood by in pained, injured innocence. Sir William was caricatured as a cuckold. Far from being received at Court, Emma was ostracised: even some of her oldest friends began to drop off. Miss Cornelia Knight, for instance, who had spent so many years with them in Italy, was advised not to live in the same hotel as the Hamiltons. Relations between Nelson and his wife steadily deteriorated. At Christmas they broke down. William Beckford, Sir William's kinsman, invited the Hamiltons and Nelson to Fonthill. They accepted. Lady Nelson, unasked, was left behind.

Emma's resilience was amazing. During their progress across Europe she had given performances of her Attitudes. In England the performances continued. At Fonthill on 23 December she presented Agrippina with the ashes of Germanicus. The spirit with which Emma could carry off such a public performance when only a month off having a secret child was the same spirit which had triumphed over her early adversities and raised her above whatever degradations she had been subjected to by poverty. Since London knew nothing of her child when she was constantly in a position of prominence, it is no wonder that her early life should be so shrouded in mystery. This, if nothing else, demonstrates that necessary discretion was second nature to her. Sir William had trusted her with State secrets; and, although she might sometimes be insensitive or over enthusiastic, she was undoubtedly trustworthy. Nelson too appreciated this. Emma had become, in his eyes, his wife, and he was loyal to her as he never had been to Fanny. He bought Merton Place, Surrey, as a home for them and their child. To Nelson for the short remainder of his life that house represented 'Paradise'. During the uneasy Peace of Amiens from April 1802 until mid-May 1803 his leave was centred on Merton. Then followed fifteen months of fatiguing responsibility, patrolling the Mediterranean. On 20 August 1805 he returned to Merton and spent what were to be his last three weeks on shore there. He left for the last time on Friday 13 September. At the Battle of Trafalgar on 21 October 1805 he died, leaving Emma as a bequest to the Nation. The days of her power were over.

89

Embroidered hem with the
motifs 'Nelson – Bronte – Nelson'
muslin embroidered with silk, gold
threads and sequins by Sicilian
embroideresses
12 x 36in (30·5 x 91·5cm)
lent by the Victory Museum, Portsmouth

See Cat. No. 81.
The weather was gloomy when they landed at Great Yarmouth on 6 November
1800, but the people flocked out to see the Hero of the Nile and both he and
Emma were prepared to make a public appearance. She was wearing her dress
embroidered with the legends 'Nelson Bronte Nelson'; and she stood with the
Admiral on the balcony of the Wrestlers' Arms acknowledging cheers in the
drizzling rain. (Tours, p. 160.)

90

Isaac Cruikshank (1756 or 7–1810)
A Mansion House Treat, or
Smoking Attitudes!
colour aquatint,
$9\frac{1}{4}$ x $13\frac{3}{4}$in (23·5 x 35cm)
inscribed in plate (conversations):
'*Yes Sir Dilbery these fighting Tars make a
cursed deal more smoke than we do.*'
'*Why Sir Dilbery, your pipe is too short, 'tis
quite worn out, it wants a new tip.*'
(Sir William) '*Aye my Lord but then they
have a cursed deal more fire too – twig the
Admiral.*'
(Pitt) '*I'll smoke the Cits again with
another Loan very soon. Very fine Virginia my
Lord.*'
(Emma) '*Pho the old man's pipes allways
out, but yours burns with full Vigour.*'
(Nelson) '*Yes Yes I'll give you such a smoke.*
I'll pour a whole broadside into you.'
(beneath print, in the plate)
*Pub. Nov. 18 1800 by S. W. Fores No.
50 Picadilly
A Mansion House Treat: or Smoking
Attitudes! I. Cks. . . . 18 November
1800/Cruickshanks*
lent by the Trustees of the British Museum

LIT: Tom Pocock, *Nelson and his World*, London, 1968, *Repr.*
News of Emma's affair with Nelson reached the London print-shops almost as
soon as the trio set foot in the capital. They arrived on Sunday 9 November.
Only nine days later this malicious caricature by Isaac Cruikshank (father of
the more famous George) was published. Emma is shown smoking, far from the
pursuit of a lady: but the sexual connotations are even more damning.

91

Thomas Rowlandson (1756–1827)
Lady H xxxxxx Attitudes
etching, trimmed to etched outline,
9⅜ x 6¾in (23·9 x 17·2cm)
inscribed (on artist's folder within
plate) : *Lady H xxxxxx Attitudes*
lent by the Trustees of the British Museum

LIT: Hardwick, *Repr.*; Tom Pocock, *Nelson and his World*, London, 1968, *Repr.*
Immediately upon Emma's return to England in November 1800 gossip, parody and caricature surrounded her name. To dismay at Nelson's evident infatuation was added disappointment at, and even contempt for the waning of her once celebrated beauty. Very nearly seven months pregnant, but apparently successfully concealing the fact from all save Nelson and her mother, she merely horrified people by her girth. Her association with Nelson led to no discovery of her imminent accouchement, but to cruel reminders of her dubious past. Her vast size in this Rowlandson cartoon indicates a date late in 1800 or early 1801. The legend that in her impoverished and reckless youth she posed nude for artists had long been current. In the Fitzwilliam Museum, Cambridge, there is a manuscript note written about 1791 by Sir James Bland Burges, an Under-Secretary of State in the Foreign Department, and an apprehensive colleague of Sir William's. It must reflect general rumour: 'This Mrs. Hart, on her first coming from the country, set out as a common Prostitute in Hedge Lane. Being very handsome she was engaged by the Committee of the Royal Academy to exhibit herself naked as a model for the young Designers.' (Fitzwilliam Museum, Percival Bequest MSS., quoted by Fothergill, p. 217.) It should, however, be noted that the fame of her Attitudes was as great as that of her louche early life.

92

Richard Cosway (1742–1821)
Emma Hamilton in a classical
attitude
pencil and watercolour,
8¾ x 5½in (22·2 x 14cm)
lent by the National Portrait Gallery

PROV: Bequeathed by Captain H. W. Murray, 1938; previous history unknown.
EXH: *Angelika Kauffmann und ihre Zeitgenossen*, Bregenz, July–October 1968; Vienna, November–February 1968–9, Cat. No. 181.
LIT: Tours, *Repr.* as frontispiece.
Cruel things had been said in the newspapers about Emma's early life and attention had unkindly been drawn to the fact that she had not been received at Court (see Tours, p. 166), but of her Attitudes the consensus of opinion was high. It seems incredible that, eight months pregnant, she could have performed successfully at Fonthill during her Christmas visit in December 1800, yet here is the account given in the *Gentleman's Magazine* of April 1801 : 'Lady Hamilton appeared in the character of Agrippina, bearing the ashes of Germanicus in a golden urn, as she presented them before the Roman people, with the design of exciting them to revenge the death of her husband, who, after having been declared joint Emperor by Tiberius, fell a victim to his envy,

and is supposed to have been poisoned by his order, at the head of the forces
which he was leading against the rebellious Armenians. Lady Hamilton displayed with truth and energy every gesture, attitude, and expression of
countenance which could be conceived in Agrippina herself, best calculated to
have moved the passions of the Romans on behalf of their favourite General.
The action of her head, of her hands, and arms in the various positions of the
urn; in her manner of presenting it before the Romans, or of holding it up to the
Gods in the act of Supplication, was most classically graceful. Every change of
dress, principally of the head, to suit the different situations in which she
successively presented herself, was performed instantaneously with the most
perfect ease, and without retiring or scarcely turning aside a moment from the
spectators. In the last scene of this most beautiful piece of pantomime, she
appeared with a young lady of the company, who was to personate a daughter.
Her action in this part was so perfectly just and natural, and so pathetically
addressed to the spectators as to draw tears from several of the company. It
may be questioned whether this scene, without theatrical assistance of other
characters and appropriate circumstances, could possibly be represented with
more effect.' (Quoted by Tours, pp. 169–70.)

In this drawing by Richard Cosway Emma is wearing a dress of the high-
waisted style of the period which must have helped substantially in concealing
her pregnancy.

93
Plate VIII, B

James Gillray (1756–1815)
Dido In Despair
etching, hand coloured
plate marks
10 x 14¼in (25·5 x 36·2cm)
inscribed (in the plate, beneath the
image):
'*Ah where & a where is my gallant Sailor
gone?
He's gone to fight the Frenchmen, for
George upon the Throne
He's gone to fight ye Frenchmen, t'loose
t'other Arm & Eye
And left me with the old Antiques, to lay me
down & cry.*'
*Pub. Feby. 6th 1801 by H. Humphrey/
No. 29 St. James's Street London*

lent by the Trustees of the British Museum

LIT: Hardwick, p. 84; Naish, *Repr.*, pl. XV.
Nelson's departure for Plymouth where he was to take up a new command on
17 January 1801 was the occasion for this malicious cartoon by Gillray. English
society tattled both about Nelson's friendship for Emma and about how fat and
far from ideal Emma's figure had become. Yet no one seems to have suggested
the real reason, her pregnancy. Gillray depicts Emma in despair as Nelson's
fleet sails away leaving her in bed with the elderly and sleeping Hamilton (then

aged 70). On the floor lies a ribbon inscribed 'The Hero of the Nile'. Around is scattered a medley of semi-erotic sculpture and publications. Sir William's own intellectual, if not physical, interests are alluded to in the cartoon: in 1780 he had discovered a pagan fertility cult still practised in the province of Abruzzo. After further research he sent his account to the Society of Dilettanti in 1781; and on this Richard Payne Knight largely based his notorious book *An Account of the Worship of Priapus lately existing in Isernia, in the Kingdom of Naples: in two letters; one from Sir William Hamilton . . .*, London, T. Spilsbury, 1786. This publication gave Sir William's fame a further dimension so lurid in the estimation of the prudish that it was obviously still remembered when Gillray made this caricature.

94
Plate VIII, A

James Gillray (1756–1815)
A Cognocenti contemplating ye Beauties of ye Antique
etching, hand coloured
trimmed close on plate marks
13¾ x 10⅛in (35 x 25·7cm)
inscribed (in plate, beneath image):
A Cognocenti contemplating ye Beauties of ye Antique/ Pubd. Feby. 11th. 1801 by H. Humphrey 27 St. James's Street

lent by the Trustees of the British Museum

Sir William now began to suffer from the public ridicule he had so long dreaded on Emma's account. Fifteen years before when Charles Greville had first suggested sending Emma out to Naples Sir William had replied 'It would be fine fun for the young English travellers to endeavour to cuckold the old Gentleman their Ambassador, and whether they succeeded or not would surely give me uneasiness.' (B.M., Add. MSS. 42071 fo. 4.) Now society mocked him for being betrayed by Emma and his own friend, Nelson. In the caricature the paintings on the wall above Sir William's head make the point: Cleopatra (Emma clutching a gin bottle), Mark Anthony (Nelson), Vesuvius and Claudius with an antlered deer (the horns of the cuckold) carved above the frame. By this time Emma had given birth secretly in Sir William's Piccadilly house, to Horatia. The day was 28 or 29 January. Within a week the baby had been sent away to a wet nurse.

95

Letter from Emma Hamilton to Mrs Gibson
autograph MS. in ink
7 x 10in (17·8 x 25·5cm)
lent by the National Maritime Museum, Greenwich

Mrs Gibson lived at 9 Great Titchfield Street which was on the rural outskirts of Marylebone. To her Emma took Horatia. Twenty-seven years later Mrs Gibson's daughter Mary told Horatia's brother-in-law, Captain Philip Ward, what she remembered of the event. 'Lady Hamilton brought the child to her mother's house in a hackney coach one night, and placed her under her charge telling her that she should be handsomely remunerated. She was unattended and did not give the nurse any information as to the child's parents. The nurse declared she was no more than eight days old. This was either in the month of January or February 1801; and Mrs Gibson said she could never make out why Horatia's birthday was kept in October. She remained with the nurse till she was 5 or 6 years old. Lady Hamilton constantly visited her: Lord Nelson was frequently her companion in her visits to her, and often came alone, and played for hours with the infant on the floor, calling her his own child.' (Quoted by Hardwick, pp. 88–9.) Several short letters survive in which Emma gives Mrs Gibson instructions about the child.

96

Sir William Beechey (1753–1839)
Lord Nelson
oil on canvas, 24½ x 19in (62·3 x 48·3cm)
inscribed (on the back of the original
canvas – picture has now been relined):
*W. B. Pinxt. Presented to his beloved son
Captn. Beechey. 1830*

lent by the Leggatt Trustees

PROV: The artist; given to his son Capt Beechey, 1830; by descent through the Beechey family to G. B. Dixon, Esq, and on his death in 1956 to Mrs Margaret Dixon.

EXH: On loan to the National Portrait Gallery since 1967.

LIT: Carola Oman, *Lord Nelson*, London, 1968, *Repr.*, pl. 5, facing p. 144; Tom Pocock, *Nelson and his World*, London, 1968, *Repr.* dust cover; David Howarth, *Trafalgar, the Nelson Touch*, 1969, *Repr.* p. 63; Winifred Gérin, *Horatia Nelson*, 1970, *Repr.* facing p. 32; *Reader's Digest*, January 1971, *Repr.* p. 145; Robin Gibson and Keith Roberts, *British Portrait Painters*, 1971, p. 12, *Repr.* pl. 32.

On 2 April 1801 Nelson took part in the Battle of Copenhagen. It was won thanks to another instance of his characteristic insubordination. The Commander-in-Chief, Sir Hyde Parker, fearing that the British were being beaten, sent out the order for action to cease. Nelson, disagreeing with the judgement, clapped his telescope to his blind eye and said: 'I really do not see the signal.' Fortunately for Emma, and history, he won.

When he returned to England Emma and Sir William took him on a country holiday. For his victory Britain created him Viscount Nelson. His next assignment was to protect the Channel coast from the attack which Bonaparte was planning. He commissioned Emma to find a house that he and Sir William could share with her. She purchased Merton Place, Surrey, on Nelson's behalf in the autumn of 1801. They moved in in October, Sir William full of praise for Emma's business-like arrangements. The three spent a family Christmas there, surrounded by Nelson's relations. On 29 April the Peace of Amiens was proclaimed and Nelson could not only enjoy a year at home, but congratulate himself on having got a bargain as he watched house prices boom.

It was during his winter leave in 1801 and the subsequent happy year at home with Emma that he was able to sit for his portrait to Beechey. This is a vivid preliminary sketch which the artist retained. The finished half-length was paid for in 1802 (35gns).

97

Anonymous
Sir William Hamilton
miniature on ivory,
$2\frac{11}{16}$ x $2\frac{3}{16}$in (6·8 x 5·6cm)
lent by the Victory Museum, Portsmouth

After the portrait now in the collection of the Duke of Hamilton. That portrait was, according to the engraving made after it by W. T. Fry, and published by Cadell and Davis on 27 March 1817, made at Naples by C. Grignon. A lock of hair is enclosed at the back of the frame of this miniature: it is a rich dark brown in colour. Sir William died on 6 April 1803.

98

Henry Bone (1755–1834)
Lady Hamilton
miniature on ivory,
$3\frac{1}{2}$ x 3in (8·9 x 7·7cm)
lent by the Victory Museum, Portsmouth

From the wording of Sir William Hamilton's now famous codicil to his will, one part of which bequeaths his Bone miniature of Emma to Nelson, it is obvious that he only possessed one miniature of her by this artist. It seems equally certain that that miniature is the one now in the Wallace Collection. (See notes on Cat. No. 50.) The present miniature shows Emma as she must have appeared in the first few years of the nineteenth century at the time that Nelson acquired Merton Place.

99
Plate vi, c

? Norsti
Mrs Cadogan
miniature on ivory
framed in blue enamel
3 x $2\frac{1}{2}$in (7·6 x 6·4cm)
inscribed
(at lower left) *? Norsti*
(around frame) *I.A.T.N.C.E.C.S.C.*
lent by the Victory Museum, Portsmouth

LIT: Hardwick, *Repr.* facing p. 72; Gérin, *Repr.* facing p. 158.
Mrs Cadogan was the name which, for reasons unknown to posterity, was assumed by Emma's mother, Mary Lyon, née Kidd. This is the only known portrait of her and indicates that Emma's receding chin, the least ideal feature of her physiognomy, was inherited from her mother. The miniature appears to show a woman in her late fifties, and must have been made at about the time that Emma's mother returned to England with the Hamiltons and Nelson. The puzzling initials about the frame, *I.A.T.N.C.E.C.S.C.*, have been interpreted by Mollie Hardwick as the initials of her 'Nelson, Matcham and Bolton "neices" and "nephews" – Eliza, Charlotte, Sarah, Tom, Anne, Catherine, Susannah. The "N" is inexplicable.' Mrs Hardwick omits to men-

tion that her interpretation also fails to account for the first letter at the lower left, 'I'. Moreover, it falls down on the fact that there are three Cs and only one S in the inscription.

Anonymous
100   Lord Nelson
miniature on ivory,
$3\frac{1}{8}$ x $2\frac{5}{8}$in (7·9 x 6·7cm)
lent by the Victory Museum, Portsmouth

The miniature shows Nelson on his left and unimpaired side. He wears the Star of the Bath, as well as a medal from the Neapolitan royal family. It may have been made after the Battle of Copenhagen in 1801 or 1802.

101   Needlework picture embroidered by Emma after a Sterne illustration
silk
diameter, including frame,
$14\frac{1}{4}$in. (36·2cm)
lent by the National Maritime Museum, Greenwich

PROV: the late Revd Hugh Nelson-Ward; given by him to the National Maritime Museum, Greenwich.
EXH: Loan collection of Nelson relics in aid of the *Save the Victory* fund, Spink and Sons, London, 1928, No. 8.
LIT: Hardwick, *Repr.* facing p. 137.
Emma is supposed to have worked this needlework picture after an illustration to Sterne's *Sentimental Journey*. Originally of Maria and Yorick, she adapted it to represent herself and Nelson walking, with a distant prospect of Merton Place. It must have been made during her year of ease and happiness at Merton, afforded by the Peace of Amiens. The embroidery is not very adept and cannot have been one of her regular pastimes.

102   Tea cup, saucer and plate
porcelain, Worcester
painted decorations by Thomas Baxter
lent by the National Maritime Museum, Greenwich

PROV: the late Revd Hugh Nelson-Ward.
In the last half of July 1802, during the Peace of Amiens, Sir William, Emma and Nelson set out on a journey across England and Wales. It was almost a triumphal progress. At Oxford for instance Nelson first had the freedom of the City bestowed upon him, and then both he and Sir William received the Honorary Degree of Doctor of Civil Law. At Milford Haven Sir William's hopes were fulfilled by Nelson's declaring it ideal for a port, thereby giving his blessing to Sir William's plans for developing it commercially.

On the long journey home they visited Worcester and there ordered this breakfast service for Merton. The symbol of paired turtle doves must have appealed more to Emma and Nelson than to Sir William. It was probably in Worcester that they met young Thomas Baxter and invited him to visit Merton.

103   Snuff box with portrait of Emma
tortoise-shell, with miniature on
ivory inset
3¼ x 2½in (8·3 x 6·4cm)
lent by the National Maritime Museum,
Greenwich

Attributed to Thomas Baxter
(1782–1821)
104   Horatia standing on a chair
pencil, 5½ x 4in (14 x 10·2cm)
inscribed (lower left):
Horatia Nelson
lent by the National Maritime Museum,
Greenwich

PROV: J. H. F. Walter.
LIT: Gérin, *Repr.* facing p. 94.
Thomas Baxter, born in Worcester, had naturally begun his career by painting on porcelain at the Worcester factory. He was 20 when the Hamiltons and Nelson met him during their tour of the west of England in 1802. He probably visited Merton soon afterwards. Although the various drawings of Horatia as a child of 3 or 4 bear little resemblance to the style of landscapes and interiors made by Baxter at Merton, they have always been associated with his name. Horatia frequently visited Merton. Nelson was anxious that she should be installed there as soon as possible, but it was not until after the death of Sir William that Emma seems to have considered taking the child there on a permanent basis.

Thomas Baxter (1782–1821)
105   Card Party at Merton
pen, ink and wash,
4 x 5in (10·2 x 12·7cm)
lent by the National Maritime Museum,
Greenwich

PROV: J. H. F. Walter.
LIT: Hardwick, *Repr.* facing p. 184.
Merton Place was a comfortable, convenient and very up-to-date mansion (each of the principal bedrooms, for instance, had its own water-closet); Emma was a good and eager hostess. The house was constantly filled with people, particularly Nelson's relations. Evidently the amusements included all those for which Emma had become famous, or infamous, in Naples and Palermo. Cards had been one of the pastimes about which Nelson's friends had remonstrated. Thomas Troubridge wrote to Nelson in 1799: 'I know you can have no pleasure sitting up all night at cards; why then sacrifice your health, comfort, purse, ease, everything to the customs of a country where your stay cannot be

long. Lady Hamilton's character will suffer; nothing can prevent people talking. A gambling woman, in the eyes of an Englishman, is lost.' (Quoted by Mollie Hardwick, p. 62.) Unfortunately Emma continued to gamble in England, playing cards not only with Nelson's female relatives.

	Thomas Baxter (1782–1821)
106	**Merton Garden**
	pen, ink and wash,
	5 x 16in (12·7 x 40·7cm)
	inscribed (in pencil lower r): *1805*

lent by the National Maritime Museum, Greenwich

PROV: J. H. F. Walter.

Emma continued to improve Merton inside and out: it kept her occupied during Nelson's long absence from mid-May 1803 until his last brief return in August 1805. When she first found the house for Nelson the grounds were charming even in Sir William's estimation – and judging from the English Garden at Caserta his standards were very high indeed.

	Thomas Baxter (1782–1821)
107	**Merton Place**
	pen, ink and wash,
	5 x 16in (12·7 x 40·7cm)
	inscribed (in pencil lower r): *1805*
	lent by the National Maritime Museum, Greenwich

PROV: J. H. F. Walters.

Nelson enjoyed only a year in England during the Peace of Amiens. When war once more broke out he was appointed to the Mediterranean command with *Victory* as his flagship. In mid-May 1803 he once more left home. Sir William had died on 6 April that year, so Nelson's departure must have left Emma more forlorn than usual; she begged Nelson to allow her to follow him to the Mediterranean. He forbade her to do so. Instead his letters are full of plans about Merton, and he encouraged her to develop things there. On the page beneath this drawing is written 'House (two sides) and grounds. The little railings [which seem to be *crossed out*] may be those wh. Nelson wrote should be put to prevent Horatia tumbling in (in one of his letters while away).' Nelson had written to Emma asking that the little stream, which they had renamed 'the Nile', should be fenced off. (See Hardwick, p. 171.)

	Silver gilt cup
108	height 3½in (8·9cm)
	diameter 2¾in (7cm)
	inscribed: *To my much loved Horatia 21st.*
	August, 1805 Nelson and Bronte/Horatia

lent by the Victory Museum, Portsmouth

In February 1804, while Nelson was patrolling the Mediterranean, Emma gave birth to another daughter. The child was short lived. Its death can only have made Nelson more passionately attached to Horatia. He returned to Merton on 20 August 1805 having been at sea for fifteen months, and the following day he ordered a knife, fork and spoon for Horatia, along with this cup. It commemorates his short and last return to his family.

109   **MS. in Emma's autograph about silver gilt cup**
12 x 10in (30·5 x 25·4cm)
lent by the Victory Museum, Portsmouth

The MS. reads: '*the Victor of Aboukir/ Copenhagen & Trafalgar/ etc. etc. etc. the glorious the great &/ good Nelson Bought this/ for his Daughter/ Horatia Nelson August 30th/ 1805. She used/ it till I thought it/ proper for her to lay it by as/ a sacred relick.*   *Emma Hamilton*'

The MS on the *verso* reads: '*She is the Daughter the/ True & Beloved Daughter/ of Viscount Nelson/ and if He had lived she/ wou'd have been all/ that His Love & Fortune/ cou'd have made her/ for Nature has made Her/ perfect Beautifull good & amiable/ Her mother was too Great/ to be mentioned but her/ Father Mother & Horatia had a/ True & virtuous friend in Emma Hamilton.*'

Curiously Emma's letter accounts for the purchase of the cup on a date different from that of the inscription.

110   **Letter from Emma to the First Lord of the Admiralty (Lord Barham)**
Autograph MS. in ink, dated Feb. 3, 1806
$8\frac{3}{4}$ x $7\frac{1}{4}$in (22·3 x 18·4cm)
lent by Mr J. E. P. Grigg

PROV: John Deas Thomson (secretary to Lord Barham); Sir Edward Deas Thomson, son of the above; Mrs Henry Grigg, daughter of the above; Edward Grigg, 1st Lord Altrincham, son of the above; by descent to present owner.

This hitherto unpublished letter from Emma to the First Lord of the Admiralty typifies her characteristic generosity. It reads:

   Clarges St. Feb. 3d 1806

My Lord

Pray forgive me – but I cannot / resist writing to you in favour / of one who was protected & Esteemed / by the great & glorious Nelson / and had *he* lived Captain Staines / stood first on the list for promotion / not only that he was a good officer / but he was beloved & indeed had / been brought up by the ever to be / lamented Nelson – and in a letter / dated the 13th of October from / his Lordship says – I hope Staines // *will get the other step & be / sent out to me for his long / & faithful Services deserve it* / pray my Lord give Ear unto what / I say I have never been in / the habit of Soliciting favours / from any one perhaps your / Lordship may have heard / that I have done some good / to my Country – my attachment to / the navy my willingness when I / was ministers wife at Naples / & Palermo to do all the good // I cou'd for Sailors from Admirals / to the lowest seaman in the / fleet may find favour in your / sight for I know you are / good &

just – I never did / ask anything to be refused / for I am too proud to / solicit if I had not justice / on my side pray then good / my Lord immagine that / Nelson asks this boon from / you & you will make very / very happy the wretched / Heart Broken but grateful / Emma Hamilton.

Sir William Charles Ross
(1794–1860)
Horatia Nelson
miniature on ivory,
$4\frac{5}{8}$ x $4\frac{1}{8}$in (11·7 x 10·4cm)
lent by the Victory Museum, Portsmouth

1 1 1
Plate VI, D

LIT: Gérin, *Repr.* facing p. 250.
Emma's remarkable beauty seemed fated to die with her. Neither the first daughter, Emma Carew, born after Emma's liaison with Fetherstonhaugh, nor Horatia Nelson were great beauties. Horatia inherited her looks more from the Nelsons. This miniature was made at the time of her marriage to the Revd Philip Ward in 1822 and shows what was to develop into a rather, gaunt face with its long chin, very like her father's. Emma, who had not inherited her beauty from her mother, was never eclipsed by one of her own daughters.

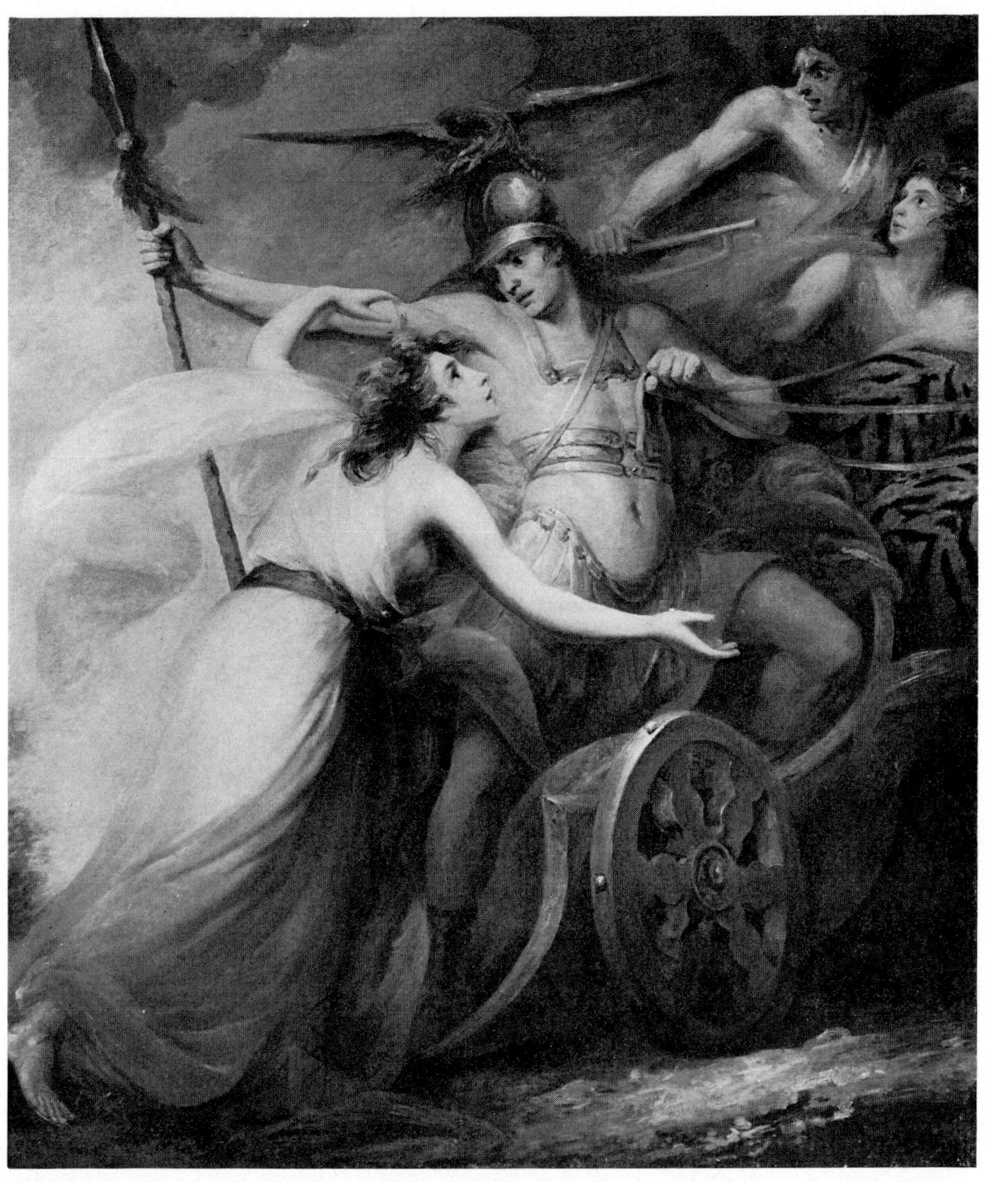

PLATE 1 *George Romney* Emma Hart as Thetis pleading with Achilles before Troy
lent anonymously (25)

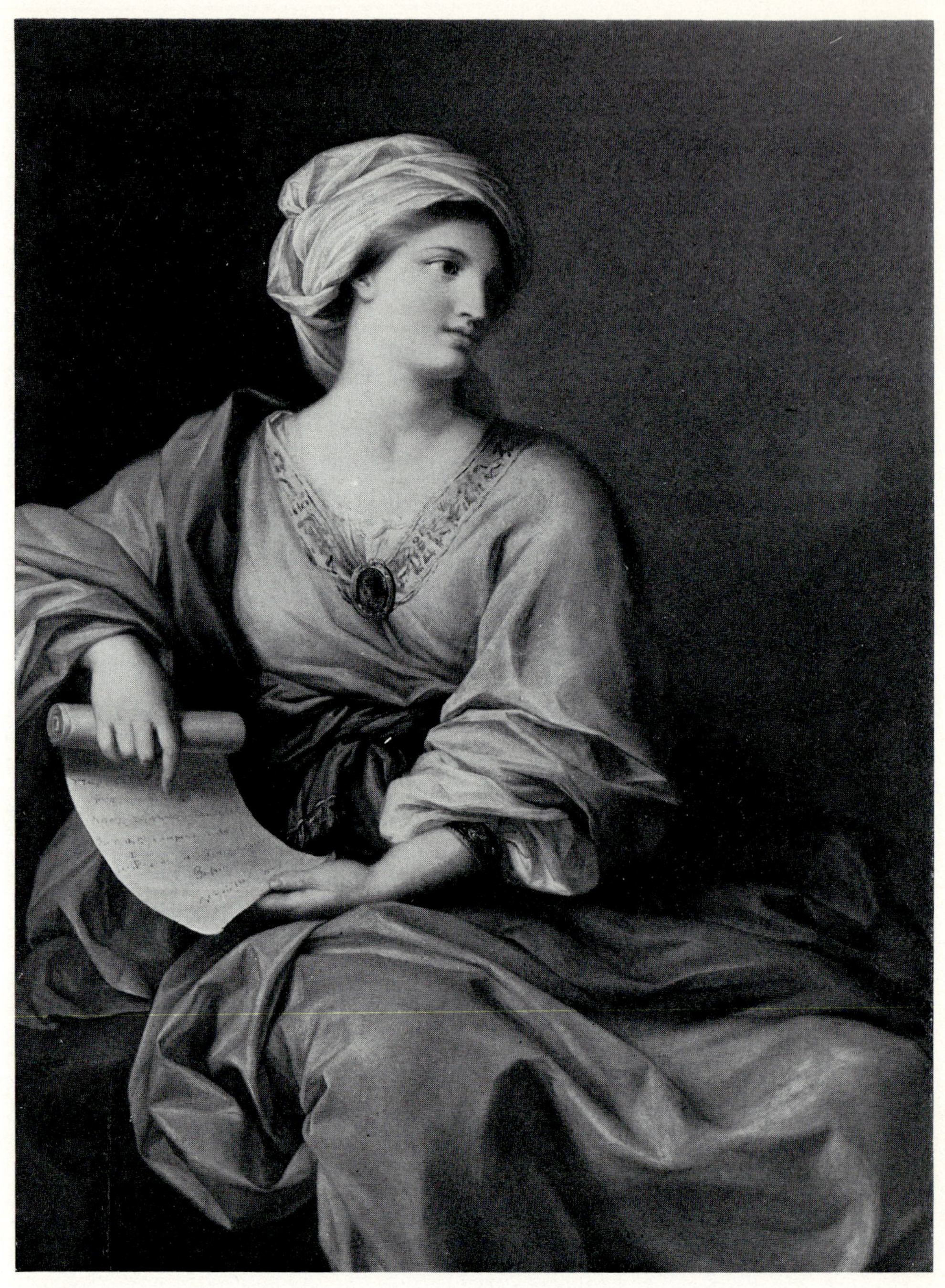

PLATE II *Gavin Hamilton* Lady Hamilton as a Sibyl
lent by Mr and Mrs Clovis Whitfield (34)

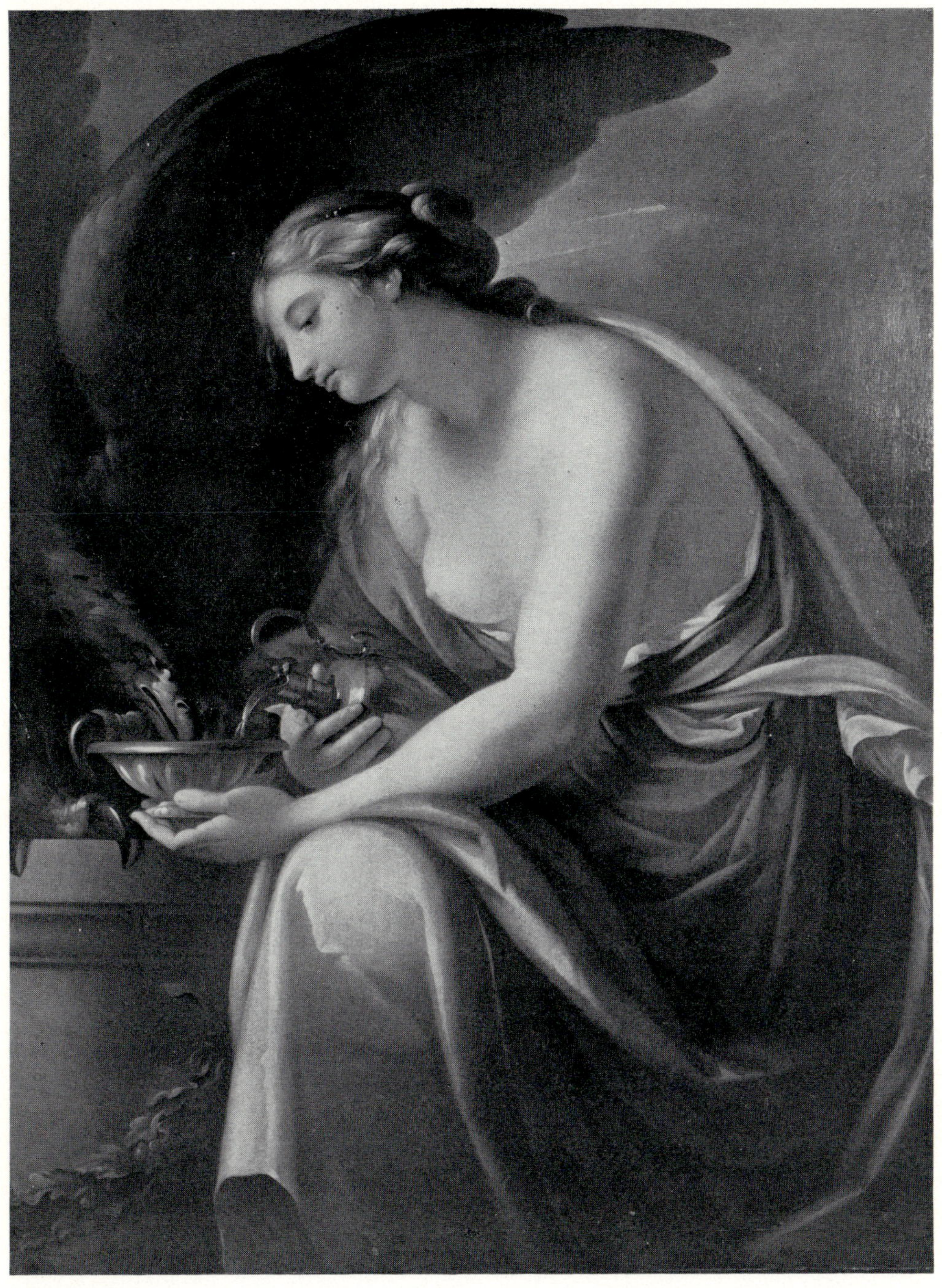

PLATE III *Gavin Hamilton* Lady Hamilton as Hebe *lent by Thomas Agnew and Sons* (35)

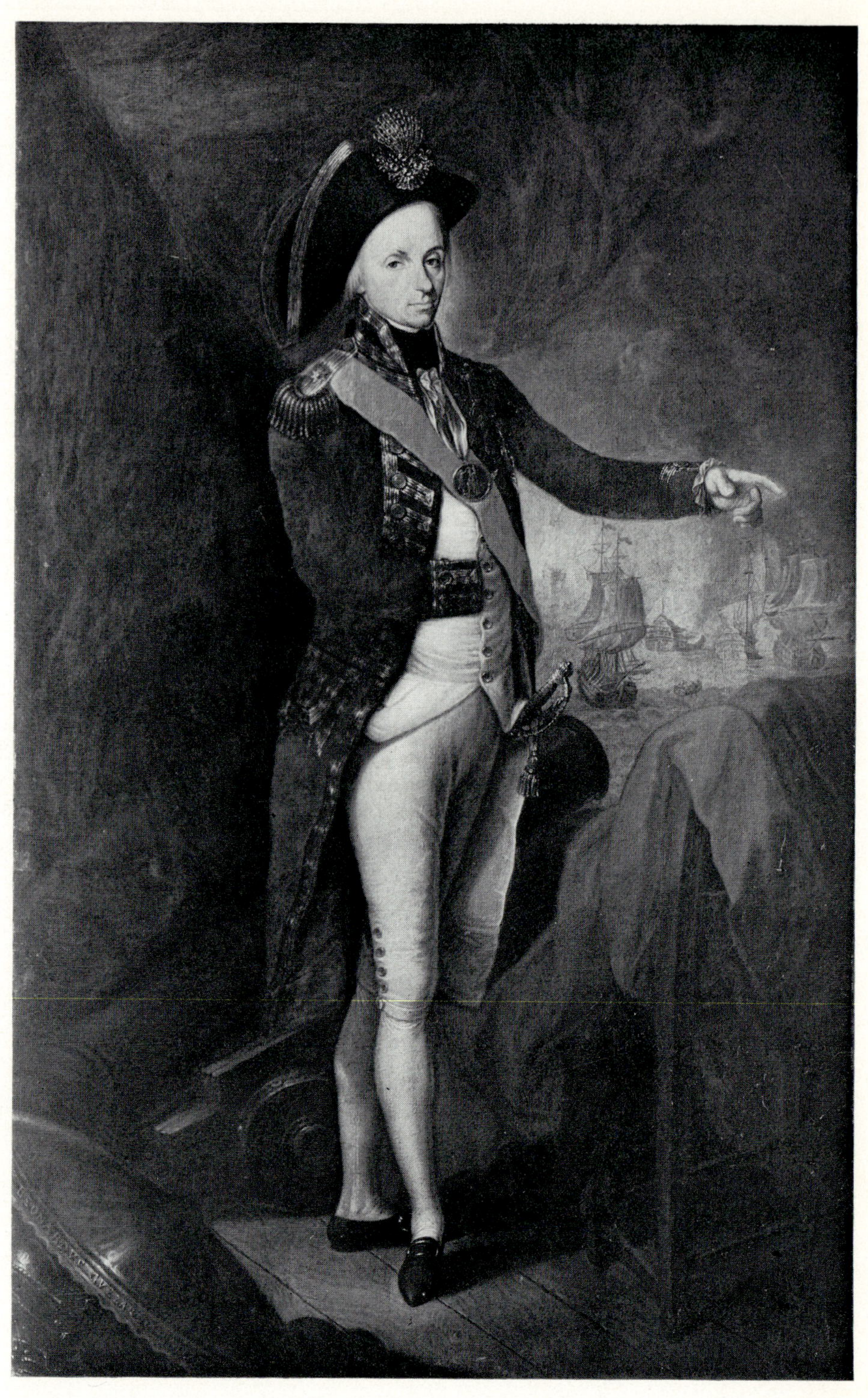

PLATE IV *Leonardo Guzzardi* Nelson *lent by the Museo di San Martino, Naples* (85)

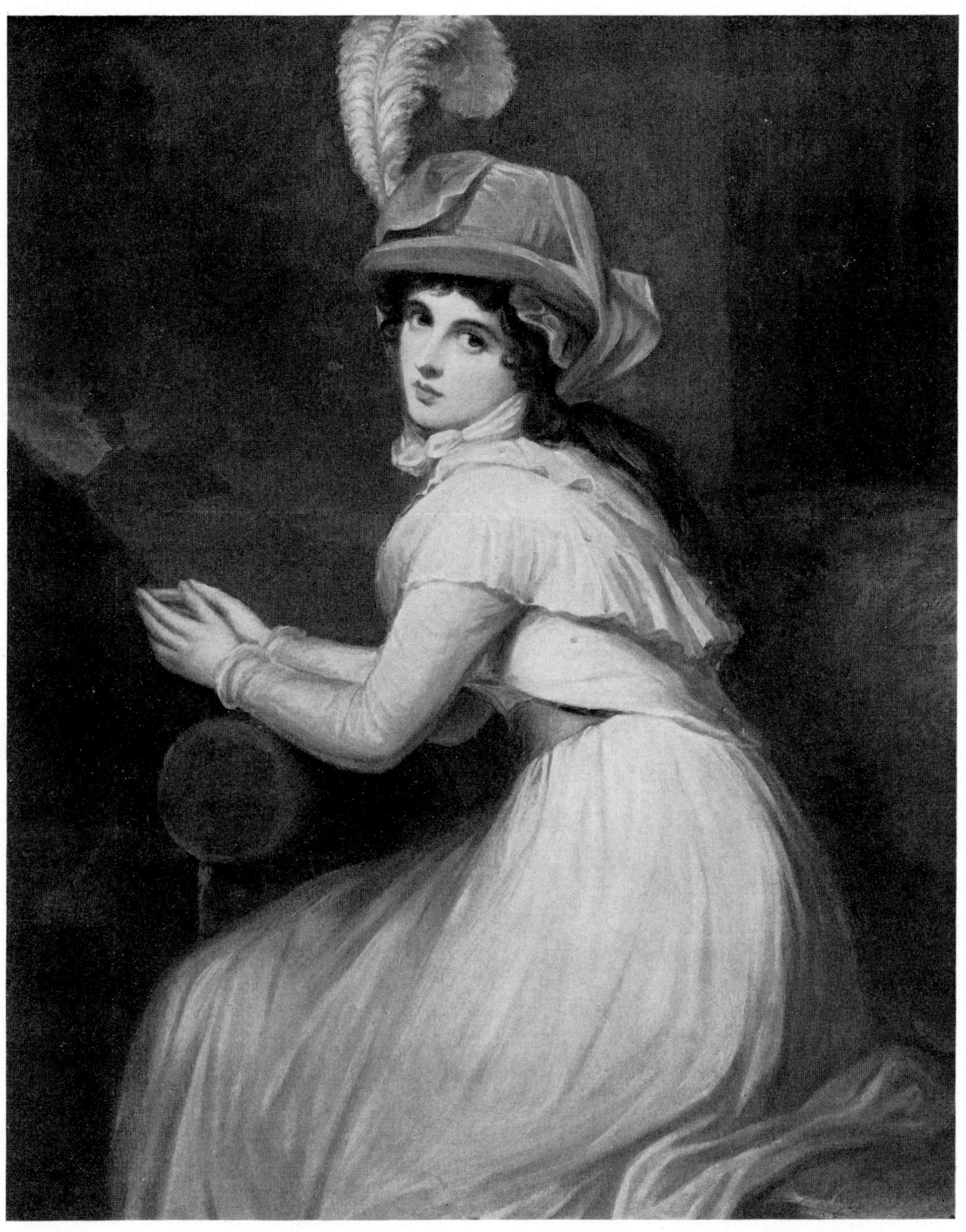

PLATE V *George Romney* Lady Hamilton as The Ambassadress
lent by Mr and Mrs Jack G. Taylor (53)

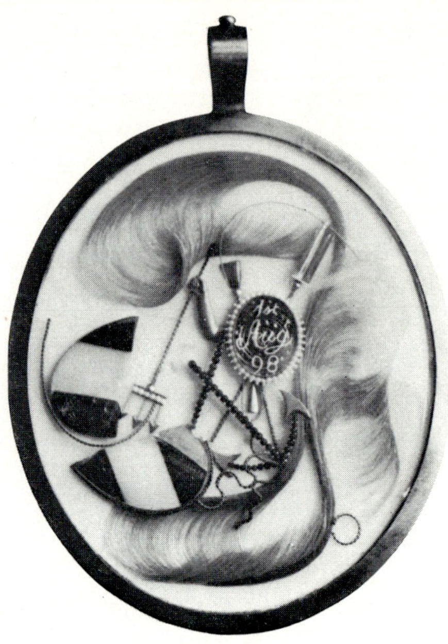

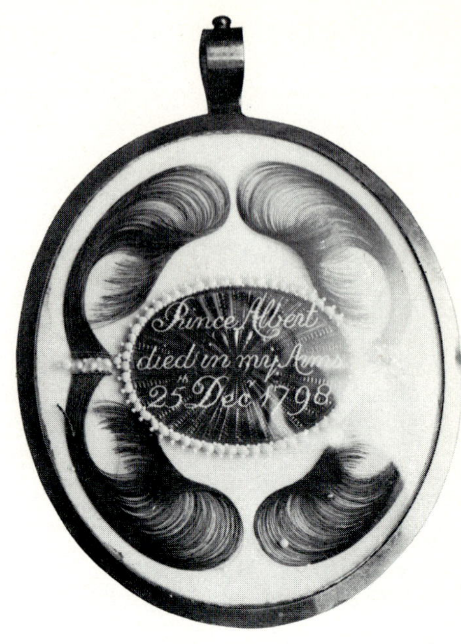

PLATE VI*a*

Memorial and mourning pendant

recto

lent by the Victory Museum
Portsmouth (75)

PLATE VI*b*

Memorial and mourning pendant

verso

lent by the Victory Museum
Portsmouth (75)

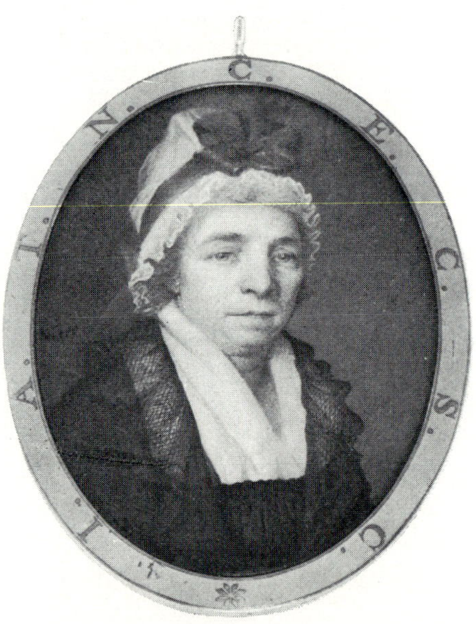

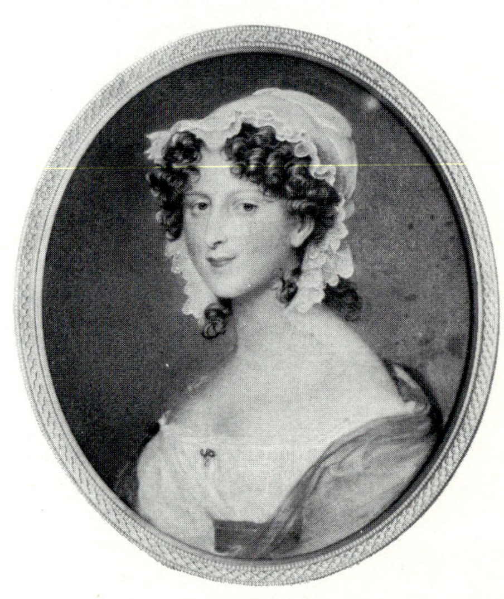

PLATE VI*c*

? Norsti Mrs Cadogan

lent by the Victory Museum, Portsmouth (99)

PLATE VI*d*

Sir William Charles Ross
Horatia Nelson

lent by the Victory Museum, Portsmouth (111)

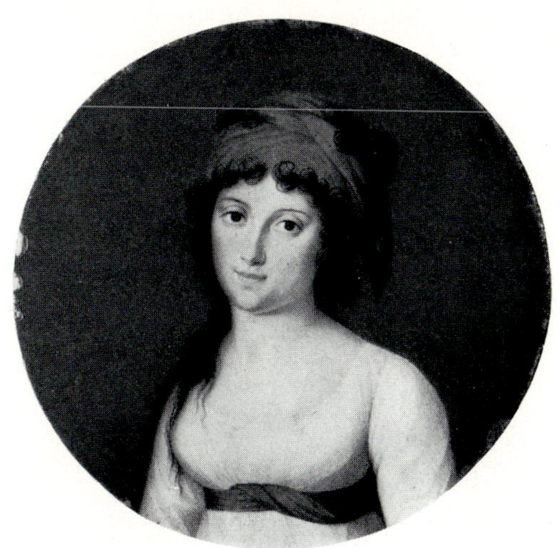

PLATE VII*a* *Selvaggi* Lucia Migliaccio, Duchessa di Floridia
lent by the Museo di San Martino, Naples (83)

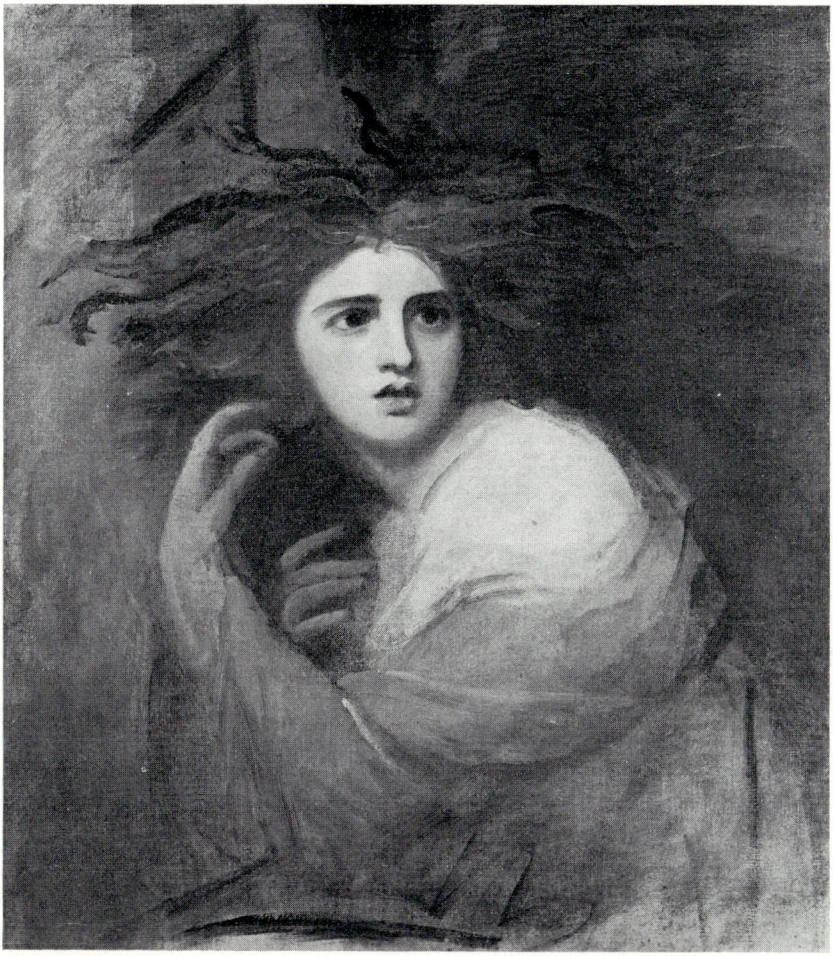

PLATE VII*b* *George Romney* Lady Hamilton as Medea
lent by the Norton Simon Foundation, Los Angeles (17)

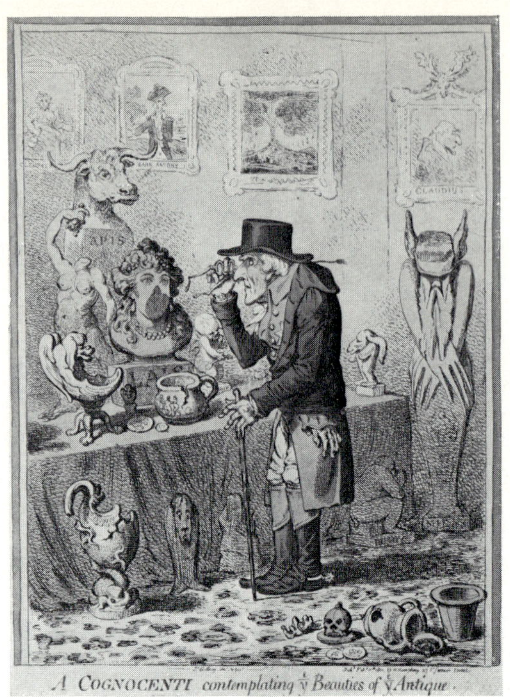

PLATE VIII*a*

James Gillray A Cognocenti comtemplating ye Beauties of ye Antique
lent by the British Museum (94)

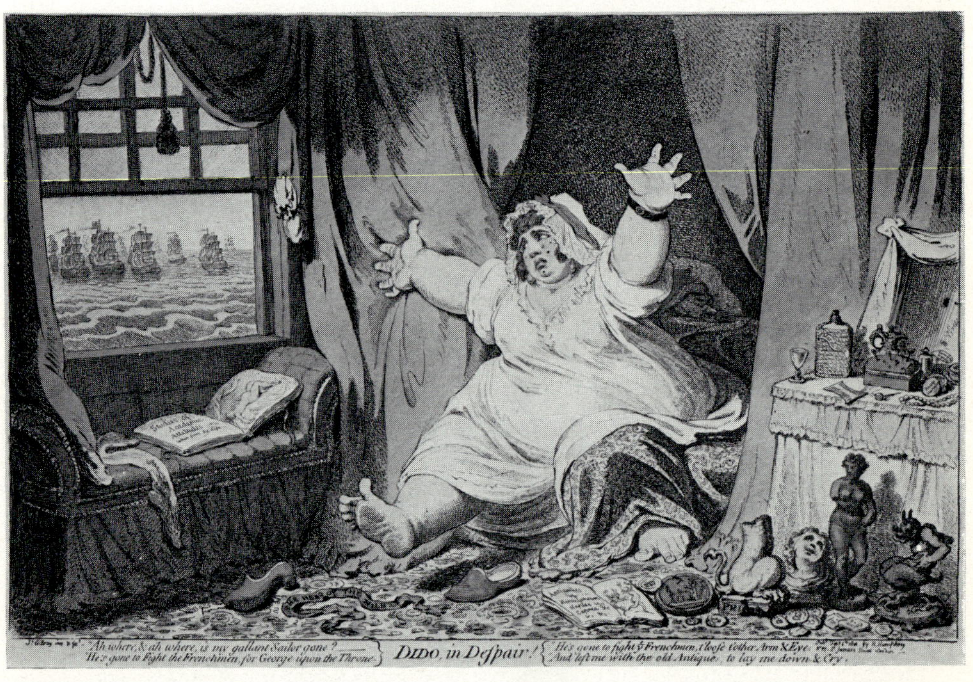

PLATE VIII*b* *James Gillray* Dido in Despair *lent by the British Museum* (93)